Essential Korean

for business use

Essential Korean for business use

First published in 2011
by Hollym International Corp., USA
Phone 908 353 1655 **Fax** 908 353 0255
http://www.hollym.com **e-Mail** contact@hollym.com

Hollym

Published simultaneously in Korea
by Hollym Corp., Publishers, Seoul, Korea
Phone +82 2 734 5087 **Fax** +82 2 730 5149
http://www.hollym.co.kr **e-Mail** info@hollym.co.kr

ISBN: 978-1-56591-312-7
Library of Congress Control Number: 2011930277

Printed in Korea

* The romanization of Korean expressions was done according to the system instituted by the Ministry of Culture and Tourism of Korea in 2000.

Essential Korean

for business use

Kwon Sungmi & John M. Frankl

Hollym

Introduction

In recent years, in conjunction with Korea's economic development, exchanges with countries from all over the world have also increased. As a result, Korean has become a language necessary for doing business not only for foreigners working in Korea but also for people working with companies in Korea or at international branches of Korean companies abroad.

Of course, when doing business with Koreans it is not always necessary to do so in the Korean language. Many companies will have employees skilled in English, or have interpreters when language is a problem. But in order to do effective international business, one must first understand the culture of the country and people. In this context, we hope that it aids in bringing its readers a bit closer to Koreans by broadening their understanding of Korean culture.

This book is constructed around the various situations one may encounter while conducting business, and includes numerous expressions that can be used by learners of Korean at all levels. Of course, it includes those expressions necessary for foreigners who reside in Korea and work permanently at Korean companies, but it also deals with situations required for short-term business trips. In a word, because it is composed of the actual Korean expressions most often used when doing business, we are confident that all readers will find it useful.

Many people helped with the writing of this book, and we would like to thank them all. Friends in the business world (Lee Eunkyo, Lee Myeongjin, et al.) provided valuable advice concerning actual situations and expressions, while Ms. Lee Chloe and Kim Sohyun of Hollym Corp., Publishers offered patience and support throughout the project.

Kwon Sungmi, Ph.D.
John M. Frankl, Ph. D.

The Composition and Usage of This Book

Composition

This book is composed of 15 chapters, each of which contains expressions necessary for both business and daily living. At the end of each chapter, there is a list of vocabulary related to the chapter's theme. Each chapter also contains a "Caution" section that introduces key elements of Korean culture. Most importantly, the "Caution" teaches readers Korean etiquette, thereby helping them avoid common mistakes based on cultural differences.

Explanation

All of the expressions contained in this book are provided with both a literal translation and an English equivalent. The literal translations provide help in understanding the original Korean, the word order of which is often quite different from the English.

Usage

All expressions contained in this book are also provided as downloadable MP3 files at www.hollym.co.kr. After first reading an expression aloud two or three times, one should then listen to the MP3 files and practice repeating the expression several times. Once an expression becomes comfortable, one should repeatedly practice saying it at the same time as the narrator. In this way, by progressing through reading aloud, repeating after, and finally simultaneously speaking, not only will one's pronunciation improve but also the expressions will become natural and therefore much more likely to come out spontaneously in the appropriate situations.

Contents

Introduction 004

The Composition and Usage of This Book 006

Chapter 1. A Typical Day at the Office

1 Going to Work 014

2 Getting off Work 017

3 Lunchtime 021

4 Working Late 025

5 Break Time 028

6 Vacations 032

Chapter 2. Office Machines and Facilities

1 Printer 042

2 Copy Machine 045

3 Office Supplies 048

4 Maintenance 052

5 Security 055

6 Deliveries 057

Chapter 3. Reports

1 Reporting Progress 066

2 Reporting Results 072

3 Reporting Market Research 075

4 Reporting on Rival Companies 078

5 Reporting Business Prospects 081

6 Presentations 084

7 Receiving Approval 087

8 Reports 090

Chapter 4. Meetings

1 Preparing for Meetings 098
2 Beginning a Meeting 100
3 Exchanging Opinions 102
4 Questions and Differing Opinions 106
5 Directing and Completing Business 109

Chapter 5. Business Telephone Calls

1 Making Calls 116
2 Receiving Calls 120
3 Leaving Messages 126
4 Taking Messages 128
5 Relaying Messages 130
6 Ending Calls 132
7 Bad Connections 134

Chapter 6. Computers and the Internet

1 Computers 140
2 Creating Documents 143
3 Homepages 145
4 Searches 148
5 Using Email 150

Chapter 7. Negotiations and Contracts

1 Introducing a Company 156
2 Visiting Factories 160
3 Explaining Products 163
4 Negotiating Price 166
5 Signing Contracts 171

Chapter 8. Office Interactions

1 Intercom Broadcasts 178
2 Icebreaking 179

3 Requesting Help 180
4 Refusals 184
5 Complaining 186

Chapter 9. Customer Service

1 Waiting on Customers 192
2 Serving Refreshments 194
3 Dealing with Orders 197
4 Order Changes, Exchanges, and Refunds 200
5 Delivery Delays · Payment Problems 203
6 Warranties and After Service 206

Chapter 10. Business Trips

1 Directing Business Trips 210
2 Requesting and Approving Business Trips 214
3 Business Trip Reports 216
4 Transportation 219
5 Hotels 223

Chapter 11. Entertaining Customers

1 At the Airport 232
2 Tour Guides 238
3 Buying Meals 240
4 Drinking 242
5 Gifts 248
6 Expressing Thanks 250

Chapter 12. Personal Relations

1 Congratulations 256
2 Encouragement · Condolences 259
3 Invitations 262
4 Gatherings 266

5 Congratulatory Messages 269
6 Messages of Condolences 273

Chapter 13. Money Matters

1 Using Credit Cards 278
2 ATMs 282
3 Salary·Bonuses 286
4 Special Pay 290
5 Calculating Expenses 292
6 Savings 294

Chapter 14. Local Transportation

1 Local Buses 302
2 The Subway 305
3 Taxis 309
4 Driving 313
5 Parking 317
6 Car Problems 320
7 Traffic Accidents 323
8 Traffic Regulations 326

Chapter 15. Getting Hired and the First Day on the Job

1 Looking for Work 332
2 Applications 337
3 Interviews 340
4 Notification of Acceptance 346
5 First Day of Work 349
6 Introducing Colleagues 352

Appendix 358

1 Going to Work

2 Getting off Work

3 Lunchtime

4 Working Late

5 Break Time

6 Vacations

CHAPTER 01

A Typical Day at the Office

Going to Work 01

Most Korean companies begin their work day at 9a.m., which makes traffic extremely heavy from the hours of 8 to 9a.m. As a result, many choose to arrive one or two hours early and invest in themselves by going to the gym or to a foreign language institute. In the past, employees had to check in at their respective departments, but now many companies employ a centralized system—a photo ID card that displays each employee's name, department, position, etc. The ID contains a smart chip, which also serves as a door key, and is thus sometimes also called a pass or a security card.

A **안녕하세요?**
be well
Good morning/afternoon/evening.

B **네, 좋은 아침입니다.**
yes good morning be
Good morning.

안녕하십니까?
be well
Good morning/afternoon/evening.

주말 잘 보내셨어요?
weekend well spent
Did you have a good weekend?

Ⓐ 민호 씨네 회사는 출근시간이 몇 시예요?
Minho's company attendance time what time be
Minho, what time do you go to work?

Ⓑ 우리 회사는 9시까지 출근해요.
our company by nine o'clock go to work
We go to work at 9 a.m.

○ 저희 회사는 지문 인식이나 카드 확인을 통해서 출근을 확인합니다.
our company through fingerprint recognition or card identification attendance check
Our company takes attendance using either fingerprint recognition or a card.

○ 요즘은 출근부 작성하게 하는 회사는 별로 없어요.
lately attendance book letting record company almost there not be
These days there are very few companies that use a written attendance record.

○ ID 카드를 안 가져 왔어요.
ID card not brought
I didn't bring my ID card.

A 몸이 안 좋아서 병원에 들렀다가 조금 늦게 출근하겠습니다.
body not good hospital stop by a little late will go to work
I am not feeling well, so I am going to the hospital before work and will be a bit late.

B 많이 안 좋나 보군요. 일 보고 천천히 들어오세요.
a lot seem not good work conduct and slowly enter
You really must be sick. Take your time and come it when you feel better.

- **셔틀버스를 놓치는 바람에 늦었습니다. 죄송합니다.**
shuttle bus because miss be late sorry
I'm late because I missed the shuttle bus. I am sorry.

- **오늘 출근길에 사장님을 만났어요.**
today on the way to work president met
Today, on my way to work, I met the president.

- **저는 출퇴근할 때 지하철에서 주로 DMB를 봐요.**
when I go to work and leave work on subway mainly DMB watch
On my way to and from work, I usually watch DMB.

Getting off Work 02

The work day of most Korean companies ends at 6 or 7 p.m. Leaving exactly at the official ending time is referred to as "칼퇴근," which literally means "knife leaving work," the knife alluding to the sharp cut between work and private time. But even after the work day has officially ended, many employees are careful not to leave while their superiors are still working.

A **김 과장님은 주로 몇 시에 퇴근하세요?**
manager Kim usually at what time leave work
Ms./Mr. Kim, what time do you usually get off work?

B **저는 보통 6시에 퇴근해요.**
I usually at six o'clock leave work
I usually leave at 6 p.m.

퇴근시간이 몇 시예요?
leaving time what time be
What time does work finish?

오늘 몇 시에 끝나요?
today at what time finish
When are you/we done today?

보통 7시면 다 끝나요.
usually seven o'clock all finish
We are usually all finished by 7 p.m.

우리 회사 퇴근시간은 6시예요.
our company leaving time six o'clock be
Our company finishes at 6 p.m.

A 퇴근 안 하세요?
leaving not do
Aren't you going?

B 네, 이것만 끝내고 퇴근하려고요.
yes only this finish and leave work
Yes, I'm going to leave as soon as I finish this.

오늘은 이만 끝냅시다.
today for now let's finish
Let's call it a day.

오늘 수고했습니다.
today took trouble
You did a good job today.

벌써 퇴근시간 다 됐네요.
already leaving time almost became
It's already time to go home.

먼저 퇴근하겠습니다.
first will leave work
I'm leaving now.

먼저 들어가겠습니다.
first will go in
I'm going to leave now.

먼저 가서 죄송합니다.
first go sorry
Sorry for leaving first.

약속이 있어서 먼저 가겠습니다.
appointment there be first will go
I have an appointment so I'll be leaving now.

A 수고하셨습니다.
efforts did
Good job.

B 조심해서 들어가십시오.
carefully please go in
Take care.

- **내일 뵙겠습니다.**

  tomorrow will see

  See you tomorrow.

- **오늘은 정시 퇴근이네요.**

  today fixed time leaving be

  We're getting off on time today.

- **외근 갔다가 거기서 바로 퇴근하겠습니다.**

  outside duty went from there straight will leave work

  I'll be working outside the office and go home straight from there.

- **수고하세요.**

  take effort

  See you later.
  Have a good day.

Why Do Korean People Ask about Age?

Koreans, after meeting someone only a few times, or sometimes even for the first time, have a tendency to ask about age. This is because speakers of the Korean language essentially require this knowledge in order to address each other with the right terms and in the proper register. Still, this can be a touchy subject even among Koreans, which has also given rise to many indirect ways of inquiring about a person's age. Asking about a person's zodiac sign, for just one example, is actually a way to ascertain his or her age. So is asking when someone entered university.

Lunchtime 03

For those who work at Korean companies, lunchtime is much more than just a time to eat. Workers gain a sense of camaraderie from eating together, while also sharing information about matters in and outside the office. Lunch in Korea begins sometime between 12 and 1p.m., and usually lasts for one hour. Most workers finish eating in 30 minutes, then spend the remaining time taking walks, working out, reading, or shopping on the Internet. Larger companies have cafeterias, making lunch even more convenient. Most people, however, choose to eat at nearby restaurant, and very few actually pack their own lunch. At high-security firms, food delivery is not allowed, but at many smaller companies' employees can have food delivered to the office.

A **김 부장님, 식사하러 안 가세요?**
manager Kim to eat not go
Ms./Mr. Kim, aren't you going to eat?

B **어, 벌써 점심시간이네요.**
uh already lunch time be
Wow, it's already lunch time.

아직 식사 안 하셨으면, 저희하고 같이 가세요.
yet eat not did with us together let's go
If you haven't eaten yet, please join us.

자, 밥 먹으러들 안 가십니까?
well meal to eat not go
Hey, aren't you (all) going to eat?

자, 밥 먹고 합시다.
well meal eat and let's do
Let's do this after we eat.

식사하셨어요?
ate
Have you eaten?

저, 오늘은 약속이 있습니다.
well today appointment there be
I have an appointment today.

A 점심 뭐 먹을까요?
lunch what shall eat
What shall we have for lunch?

B 구내식당에서 먹을까요?
at cafeteria shall eat
Shall we eat at the cafeteria?

오늘 점심 어디서 먹을까요?
today lunch where shall eat
Where shall we eat today?

중국 음식 시켜 먹을까요?
Chinese food shall order and eat
Shall we order Chinese food?

오늘 구내식당 메뉴가 뭐예요?

today cafeteria menu what be

What are they serving at the cafeteria today?

오늘은 부대찌개 먹을까요?

today *budae jjigae* shall eat

Shall we have *budae jjigae* today?

저는 도시락 싸 왔어요.

I lunch box packed and came

I packed my lunch.

일이 많아서 간단히 사다 먹을 거예요.

work a lot simply will buy and eat

I have a lot of work. I'll just buy something and eat it here.

김밥으로 대충 때우려고요.

with *gimbap* roughly make do

I'm just going to have a little *gimbap*.

○ **구내식당이 지겨운데 오늘은 나가서 먹을까요?**

cafeteria tired today shall go out and eat

I'm sick of the cafeteria. Shall we go out to eat today?

○ **오늘은 배달시켜 먹을까요?**

today let deliver and eat

Shall we have something delivered today?

○ **자장면 시켜 먹을까요?**

jajangmyeon shall order and eat

Shall we have *jajangmyeon* delivered?

○ **근처에 삼계탕 잘하는 집 아세요?**

near *samgyetang* do well house know

Do you know of anywhere nearby that has good *samgyetang*?

○ **이 식당은 반찬이 많이 나와서 좋아요.**

this restaurant side dish many came out good

I like this restaurant because they serve a lot of side dishes.

○ **점심 먹고 나면, 식곤증 때문에 너무 졸려요.**

lunch after eating because of languor too sleepy

I get really sleepy after eating lunch.

04 Working Late

Korean office workers often have to stay late into the evening. They work a lot of overtime compared to those in other OECD countries. Many see this as the combination of Korean diligence, Confucian values, and the Protestant ethic that gave rise to the "Miracle on the Hangang River." Working past regular hours is alternately referred to as "시간 외 근무," "연장 근무," and "특근." And, finally, because it almost always takes place after hours, it is called "야근."

A **오늘 야근할 수 있겠어요?**
today can work night time
Will you be able to work tonight?

B **네, 오늘 밤에 별일 없습니다.**
yes tonight special thing there not be
Yes, I don't have anything planned.

죄송합니다. 집에 일이 있어서 도저히 안 될 것 같습니다.
sorry at home work there be hardly seem not possible
I'm sorry. I have something to do at home. I really don't think I can.

죄송합니다. 오늘 저녁에 약속이 있는데요.
sorry today evening appointment there be
I'm sorry. I have an appointment tonight.

Ⓐ 벌써 3일째 야근이에요.
already third night work be
This is the third night in a row I've worked late.

Ⓑ 힘냅시다.
strength put out let us
Let's cheer up.

마무리할 업무가 있어서 오늘은 야근합니다.
round off duty there be today work night
I'm working late tonight because there's something I have to finish.

오늘도 야근이네요.
today also night work be
I'm working late again tonight.

오늘도 밤샘 근무네요.
today also all-night work be
We'll be working all night again.
We're pulling anohter all-nighter.

Ⓐ 퇴근 전까지 끝낼 수 있을까요?
before leaving can finish
Will we be able to finish before quitting time?

Ⓑ 좀 어려울 것 같은데요.
a little seem hard
It may be a bit difficult.

오늘 제가 당직이에요.
today I on call be
I'm on duty today.

우리 부서는 연장 근무를 별로 안 하는 편이에요.
our department extension work almost tend not do
Our department has relatively little extended work.

우리 회사는 너무 자주 야근해요.
our company too often work nights
At our company we work too many nights.

밤샘 근무는 역시 힘들어요.
all-night work as expected hard
Pulling an all-nighter really is hard.

야식 시켜 먹을까요?
night food shall order and eat
Shall we order a late-night snack?

밤참 좀 먹을까요?
night food a little shall eat
Shall we have a late-night snack?

Break Time 05

Most companies do not have actually scheduled break time. But employees are free to take short breaks from work in order to have coffee or tea, smoke a cigarette, or chat. But smoking must usually be done outside, especially in larger buildings that have no designated smoking area. Even when there are smoking areas, smoking in shared spaces such as stairwells or hallways may result in fines. Most recently, as they begin to understand the positive relationship between employee health and productivity, companies are taking the lead in reducing the number of smokers among their employees.

A **잠깐 쉬었다가 할까요?**
little break shall take
Shall we take a little break?

B **그럴까요?**
shall do so
Shall we?

좀 쉬어가면서 합시다.
a little take rest let's do
Let's take some breaks while we work.

커피 한 잔 할까요?
coffee one cup shall do
Shall we get a cup of coffee?

차 한 잔 할까요?
tea one cup shall do
Shall we have a cup of tea?

옥상에 가서 바람 좀 쐬고 올까요?
to rooftop go wind a little shall be exposed and come
Shall we go up on the roof and get some fresh air?

A 오늘 커피믹스만 벌써 다섯 잔째네요.
today coffee-mix only already five cup be
I've already had five cups of instant coffee today.

B 커피를 너무 많이 마시면 몸에 안 좋아요.
coffee too much if drink to body not good
Too much coffee is not good for you.

녹차는 너무 오래 우리면 쓴맛이 나요.
green tea too long if soak bitter taste occur
If you steep green tea for too long, it becomes bitter.

○ **아메리카노가 마시고 싶은데, 인스턴트 커피밖에 없네요.**

Americano would like to drink nothing other than instant coffee there not be

I feel like an Americano, but all we have is instant.

○ **요즘 카페인을 너무 많이 섭취하는 것 같아요.**

these days caffeine too much seem consume

I think I'm consuming too much caffeine these days.

Ⓐ **담배 한 대 피고 할까요?**

cigarette one piece shall smoke and do

Shall we take a cigarette break?

Ⓑ **흡연실에서 봅시다.**

at smoking room let's see

Let's meet in the smoking room.

○ **재떨이는 어디에 있죠?**

ashtray where there be

Where's the ashtray?

○ **담배 있어요?**

cigarette have

Do you have a cigarette?

○ **라이터 있어요?**

lighter have

Do you have a lighter?

○ **불 좀 빌립시다.**

light please let's borrow

Can I get a light?

우리 회사는 건물 전체가 금연 구역이에요.

our company whole building non-smoking area be

Our entire building is a non-smoking area.

여성 전용 휴게실 있어요?

female exclusive rest room there be

Is there a female only lounge?

휴게실이 어디예요?

rest room where be

Where is the lounge?

이제 다시 일하러 갈까요?

now again to work shall go

Shall we get back to work?

Caution

Do not say "수고하세요." and "수고하셨습니다." to a superior.

These expressions can be quite productive and useful. It can be used to mean "good-bye" and "thank you" among others. When leaving a store or getting out of a taxi, it is perfectly appropriate. To a supervisor at the company, a professor, or any other person who is senior to you, however, it is quite rude.

Vacations 06

Employees may apply for regular monthly and yearly vacations, but there are also special vacations allowed for special occasions or health reasons. Yearly vacations become longer according to how long an employee has been with a company. This additional vacation time may be used for summer breaks, winter breaks, or any other way the employee wishes. Most summer breaks last between three and seven days. These are paid vacation, and some choose not to take them and receive additional pay instead. Additionally, female employees are allowed one day per month for menstrual leave. Vacations for special occasions vary; weddings are usually given five to seven days, while a death in the family is between three and seven. When additional vacations are needed, they may be given, but without pay. Of course, when workers are not feeling well, sick leave is also granted.

A **여름휴가 일정은 잡았어요?**
summer vacation schedule fixed
Have you made plans for your summer vacation?

B **8월 1일부터 7일까지로 신청하려고 해요.**
from August 1st to 7th intend to apply
I am going to apply for August 1st to 7th.

휴가 언제쯤 가실 거예요?
vacation around when will go
When are you going on vacation?

휴가 날짜는 정하셨어요?
vacation date decided
Have you decided on your vacation dates?

7월 말쯤에 휴가 갈 생각이에요.
around end of July vacation think to go
I am thinking of going on vacation around the end of July.

나중에 휴가 일정 정해서 알려 드릴게요.
later vacation schedule decide and will let know
I'll let you know later after I've decided on my vacation plans.

아내하고 의논해 봐야겠어요.
with wife will try to discuss
I have to discuss it with my wife.

A 7월 20일부터 7월 26일까지 휴가 신청해도 될까요?
from July 20th to July 26th vacation can apply
Can I apply for a vacation from July 20th to 26th?

B 여기 다른 부서원들이 제출한 휴가 신청서가 있으니까, 이거 보고 원하는 일정 체크하세요.
here other members submitted vacation application there be this see and want schedule please check
Here is the form with the other employees' requests. Have a look at it and fill in your desired dates.

7월 말에서 8월 초에는 휴가를 쓰는 사람이 많아서 휴가 받기가 어렵습니다.
from July end to August beginning vacation use person many vacation get hard
Lots of people go on vacation at the end of July and beginning of August, making it hard to go then.

- 휴가계 내려고 하는데요.

vacation application intend to submit

I'm going to submit an application for a vacation.

- 휴가계는 어디에 내야 돼요?

vacation application where should submit

Where do I submit my application for a vacation?

- 할머니께서 돌아가셔서 모레까지 출근 못 할 것 같습니다.

grandmother passed away untill the day after tomorrow cannot attend

My grandmother passed away, so I don't think I can go back to work until the day after tomorrow.

- 맹장 수술을 받게 돼서 다음 주까지 병가를 내야 됩니다.

appendix operation took untill next week sick leave should submit

I had an operation on my appendix, so I have to be on sick leave untill next week.

- 오늘 조퇴 좀 했으면 합니다.

today leave early a little want

I'd like to leave a bit early today.

- 며칠 정도 휴가 받을 수 있어요?

about how many days vacation can get

How many days of vacation can I get?

- 7일 정도 휴가 받을 수 있어요.

about seven days vacation can take

You can take about seven days off.

- 김 대리가 내일 대신 좀 봐 주세요.

supervisor Kim tomorrow instead please take care

Ms./Mr. Kim, please take over for me tomorrow.

A 언제 휴가 가실 거예요?
when vacation will go
When are you going on vacation?

B 8월 초쯤에 휴가 가려고요.
around beginning of August vacation intend to go
I plan on going around the beginning of August.

언제쯤 휴가 쓰실 계획이에요?
around when vacation plan to use
When do you plan to use your vacation?

갑자기 일이 터져서 휴가를 못 갔어요.
suddenly work break out vacation couldn't go
Something suddenly came up so I couldn't go on vacation.

일이 많아서 휴가를 못 갈 것 같아요.
work a lot vacation seem not go
I have so much work that I don't think I'll be able to go on vacation.

A 휴가는 어떻게 보내실 계획이에요?
vacation how to spend plan be
How do you plan to spend your vacation?

B 조용한 데서 쉬다 오고 싶어요.
at quiet place would like to take rest and come
I want to go somewhere quiet and get some rest.

휴가 계획 있어요?
vacation plan there be
Do you have any vacation plan?

가족들하고 괌에 놀러 가려고요.
with family to Guam intend to go play
I'm going to Guam with my family.

A 김 과장님 계세요?
manager Kim there be
Is Ms./Mr. Kim in?

B 지금 휴가 중이세요.
now in vacation
She/He is on vacation.

언제쯤 돌아오세요?
around when come back
When will she/he be back?

휴가 가셨습니다.
vacation went
She/He went on vacation.

◌ **어제부터 휴가 떠나셨어요.**

from yesterday vacation left

She/He is on vacation from yesterday.

◌ **다음 주 수요일쯤 출근하실 거예요.**

next week around Wednesday will come to work

She/He will be back to work around Wednesday of next week.

A **휴가 잘 보내셨습니까?**

vacation well spent

Did you have a nice vacation?

B **네, 푹 쉬고 왔습니다.**

yes good rest and came

Yes, it was quite restful.

◌ **휴가 재미있었어요?**

vacation interesting

Was your vacation enjoyable?

◌ **휴가가 너무 짧아서 아쉬웠어요.**

vacation too short sad

My vacation was regrettably short.

그동안 밀린 일이 많아 걱정입니다.
meantime piled-up work a lot worry
I'm worried about all the work that accumulated in my absence.

오래 쉬다가 일하려니 더 일하기 싫네요.
long time rest work more dislike to work
Working after such a long break is even harder.

A 내일 하루 휴가를 낼까 하는데요.
tomorrow one day off think to submit
I'm thinking of taking tomorrow off.

B 무슨 일이지요?
what matter be
What's the matter?

휴가계를 내도 될까요?
leave application may submit
May I sumbit an application for a vacation?

휴가계를 작성해서 오세요.
leave application please make and come
Come back after you have filled out an application for leave.

올해는 빨간 날이 너무 없어서 속상해요.
this year red day too there not be upset
I'm a bit upset at how few holidays there are this year.

이번 달에는 휴일이 없어서 무슨 맛으로 살지요?
this month holiday there not be for what taste live
How will I get motivated when there is no holiday this month?

Vocabulary

Work Positions

회장
chairman

사장
president

전무
executive director

상무
managing director

이사
director

고문
advising director

감사
auditing director

본부장
senior manager

부장
general manager

차장
deputy general manager

과장
manager

대리
assistant manager/supervisor

사원
specialist

팀장
team leader

1 Printer

2 Copy Machine

3 Office Supplies

4 Maintenance

5 Security

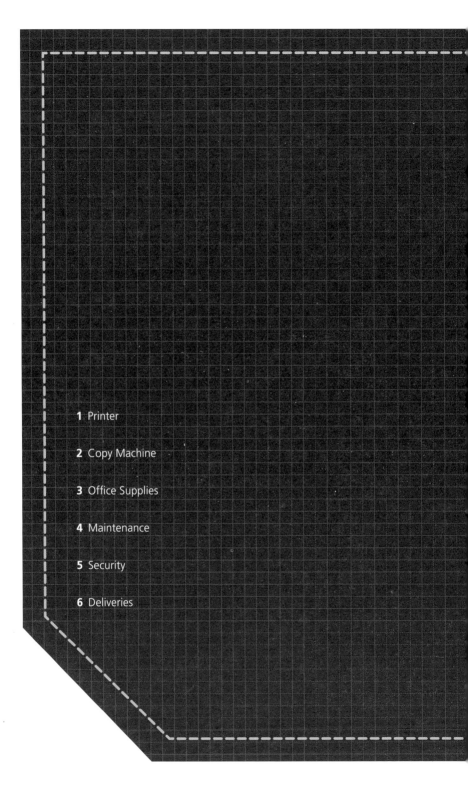

6 Deliveries

CHAPTER 02

Office Machines and Facilities

Printer 01

Most office printers are on a network that is shared by multiple users, and often the main office server must be turned on before the printer will work. As a result, whenever the printer won't work, the first thing to check is whether the server has been turned on. Also, when something fails to print, be sure to cancel it on your computer in order to avoid inconveniencing other users once it is working again.

A **프린터 출력이 안 돼요.**
printer print out not possible
The printer isn't working.

B **잉크가 다 된 것 같아요.**
ink all seem done
I think it's out of ink.

검정 잉크가 다 떨어졌네요.
black ink all ran out
It's out of black ink.

카트리지를 교체해야겠어요.
cartridge should replace
We have to replace the cartridge.

메인 컴퓨터를 켜야 다른 컴퓨터에서도 출력할 수 있어요.
main computer should turn on from other computer can print out
You have to turn on the main computer in order to print from other computers.

프린터가 연결된 컴퓨터는 항상 켜 두세요.
printer connected computer always please leave turn on
Always leave on the computer that is connected to the printer.

종이가 걸렸어요.
paper jammed
The paper is stuck.
The printer is jammed.

종이가 떨어졌어요.
paper ran out
It's out of paper.

A **너무 연하게 나왔네요. 다시 뽑아 오세요.**
too light came out again please print out
It's too light. Print it again.

B **네, 알겠습니다.**
yes understood
Okay.

- **글자가 흐릿해서 잘 안 보입니다.**
letter blurred well not seen
The letters are too light to read.

- **메인 컴퓨터에서 인쇄 명령을 취소해야 돼요.**
from main computer print order should cancel
You have to cancel your print order on the main computer.

- **이면지를 사용하면 프린터가 고장 나기 쉽습니다.**
reusable paper use printer break down easily
If you reuse paper, the printer is more likely to break.

- **한 면에 두 페이지가 나오게 출력하고 싶은데 어떻게 하는지 아세요?**
on one side two page come out would like to print out how do (you) know
I want to print two pages of text on one sheet of paper. Do you know how?

Copy Machine 02

Ⓐ **양면 복사해 오세요.**
both sides please copy and come
Make a two-sided copy.

Ⓑ **네, 알겠습니다. 그런데 몇 부 복사할까요?**
yes understood but how many copy will copy
Okay. But how many copies should I make?

축소 복사해 오세요.
please microcopy and come
Please reduce this.

확대 복사해 오세요.
please enlarge copy and come
Please enlarge this.

50부 복사해 오세요.
50 copy please copy and come
Please make 50 copies.

Ⓐ 어, 복사 용지가 없다고 나오네요.
uh copy paper there not be emerge
Uh, it says it's out of paper.

Ⓑ 트레이에 종이를 넣어야 합니다.
in tray paper should put
You have to put paper in the tray.

A4 용지가 없어요.
A4 paper there not be
There's no A4 paper.

기계를 열고 앞문을 여세요.
machine open front door please open
Open the machine, and then open the side door.

걸린 종이를 빼내세요.
jammed paper please pick out
Take out the jammed paper.

종이를 당겨내세요.
paper please pull out
Pull out the paper.

Ⓐ 복사기 어떻게 쓰는지 아세요?
copy machine how use know
Do you know how to use the copy machine?

Ⓑ 복사하려는 종이를 복사기 위에 올려놓고, 원하는 매수만 누르면 돼요.
to copy paper on copy machine put want number press
Put the paper you want to copy on top of the machine, then enter the number you want.

자동분류를 하려면 뭘 눌러야 하죠?
automatic classification do what should press
What do I have to press for automatic sorting?

복사한 거 놓고 가셨네요.
copied thing left and went
You forgot your copies.

복사한 거 놓고 가신 분 누구세요?
copied thing left and gone person who be
Who left these copies here?

Making Polite Conversation

What is the meaning behind such polite proposals as "언제 식사나 합시다." and "언제 한잔 합시다."? Are these really invitations for a meal or drink? They may be at times, but they are more often just polite conversation. If these questions are not followed by a concrete discussion of times and places, there is a high probability that they are just being used in place of a greeting. As such, when someone makes such a suggestion, rather than immediately following up with concrete questions, merely replying "네, 그럽시다." is likely more appropriate.

Office Supplies 03

Ⓐ 스카치 테이프로 붙여야겠어요.
with Scotch tape should attach
I'll have to use Scotch tape for this.

Ⓑ 제 서랍 안에 하나 있을 거예요.
in my drawer one there may be
There should be one in my drawer.

- 포스트잇에 메모해서 부장님 책상 위에 붙여 놨어요.
on Post-it take memo on manager's desk attached
I wrote it on a Post-it and stuck it to the manager's desk.

- 형광펜으로 표시한 부분은 특히 유의해서 봐 주십시오.
with highlights marked part especially please pay attention and see
Please pay particular attention to the parts marked with a highlighter.

- 이 서류는 제 서류철에 끼워 두세요.
this document in my folder please insert
Please put these papers in my file.

- 이것들은 고무줄로 묶어 두세요.
these with elastic band please tie
Please bundle these together with a rubber band.

- 펀치로 구멍을 뚫어서 바인더에 끼워 두세요.
with punch hole pierce into binder please insert
Please punch holes in these and put them in a binder.

날클립 있어요?
plate clip there be
Do you have a plate clip?

클립을 끼우는 게 낫겠어요.
clip fasten will be better
It would be better to clip them together.

월간 보고서는 링바인더에 보관하면 됩니다.
monthly report in ring binder can keep
You can keep monthly reports in a ring binder.

바인더 옆쪽에 라벨을 붙였습니다.
binder on side label attached
I put a label on the side of the binder.

편지봉투 뜯는 거 있어요?
letter envelope opener there be
Do you have a letter opener?

빈 종이 몇 장만 주세요.
blank paper some sheets only please give
Please give me a few sheets of blank paper.

포켓이 있는 폴더가 필요해요.
pocket there be folder need
I need a pocket folder.

포켓에 끼워 두세요.
in pocket please insert
Please put this in the pocket.

필기구가 없네요.
pen there not be
There's nothing to write with.

Ⓐ 스테이플러에 심이 없네요.
in stapler lead there not be
The stapler is out of staples.

Ⓑ 제 서랍에 심이 있어요.
in my drawer lead there be
There are some in my desk drawer.

- 회의 자료는 스테이플러로 찍어서 돌리세요.
meeting data with stapler please take hand out
Please staple the meeting papers together and distribute them.

- 스테이플러는 왼쪽 모서리에 찍으세요.
stapler at left corner please take
Please staple these on the left corner.

- 스테이플러 심을 뜯어내고 다시 찍어야 해요.
stapler lead remove again should take
I have to take the staple out and do it again.

- 스테이플러 뜯는 거 어디 있어요?
stapler lead remover where there be
Where is the staple remover?

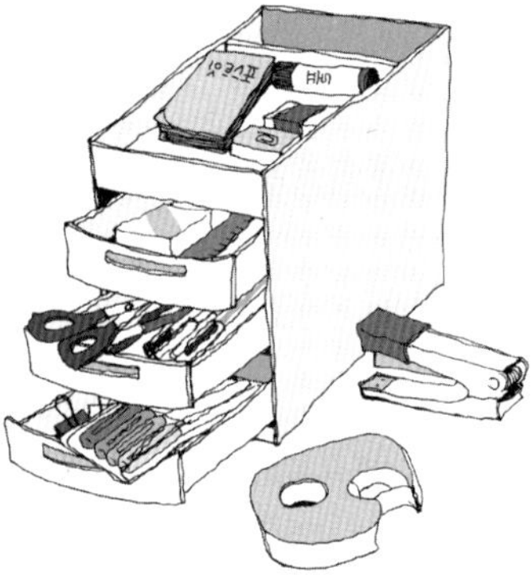

Ⓐ 문구류 주문은 어떻게 합니까?
stationery order how do
How can I order office supplies?

Ⓑ 문구류 주문은 2주에 한 번씩 담당부서에 이메일로 신청하실 수 있습니다.
stationery order in two weeks one time to the department in charge by email can apply
You can email the department in charge and request office supplies every two weeks.

펜은 색깔별로 10개씩 주문해 주세요.
pen for color ten piece each please order
Please order me ten pens for each color.

투명 파일 폴더는 넉넉하게 주문해 두세요.
clear file folder enough please order
Please order plenty of clear file folders.

문구류 카탈로그를 보고 주문하시면 됩니다.
stationery catalog see can order
You can look at the office supply catalog and make your order.

문구 구매 거래처가 변경되었습니다.
stationery purchase trade changed
The place we buy our office supplies changed.

Maintenance 04

When a building has an office in charge of all maintenance, you may go there to ask for assistance. When it does not, you should take care of small things like changing a light bulb yourself, while going for the equipment suppliers and manufacturers for after service and other larger maintenance concerns.

A **여기 전구가 나간 거 같아요.**
here bulb seem ran out
I think this light bulb is burnt out.

B **관리실에 전화해 볼게요.**
to maintenance office will call
I'll call the maintenance office.

난방이 안 됩니다.
heating not possible
The heater's not working.

히터가 안 됩니다.
heater not work
The heater won't work.

불이 안 들어와요.
fire not come in
The heat won't come on./The light(s) won't turn on.

○ **너무 추운데 온도 좀 올려 주세요.**
too cold temperature please raise
It's too cold. Please turn up the temperature.

○ **너무 더운데 온도 좀 낮춰 주세요.**
too hot temperature please lower
It's too hot. Please lower the temperature.

○ **문이 고장 나서 안 열려요.**
door break down not open
The door is broken. It won't open.

○ **온수가 안 나와요.**
hot water not come out
The hot water is broken./There's no hot water.

○ **변기가 막혔어요.**
toilet clogged
The toilet is clogged.

○ **변기에 물이 넘치고 있어요.**
at toilet water overflowing
The toilet is overflowing.

A 복사기가 완전히 고장 났습니다.
copy machine completely broke down
The copier is completely broken.

B 일단 고장 메모를 붙이세요.
once out of order memo please attach
First, put a note on it saying it's broken.

- A/S하는 곳에 전화하세요.
  to after service place please call
  Please call the service center.

- 수리 기사를 불렀습니다.
  repair mechanic called
  I called a repairman.

- 무상서비스 기간이라 무료로 A/S를 받을 수 있습니다.
  free service period for free after service can get
  It's still under warranty, so we can get free after service.

- 출장서비스를 부르면 수리비 말고 출장비를 별도로 2만원 내야 합니다.
  away service if call excluding repairing cost traveling expense for extra 20,000 won should pay
  If we have someone come here, the repair is free but there is an additional outcall charge of 20,000 won.

Security 05

Ⓐ 누구를 만나러 오셨나요?
who to meet came
Who are you here to see?

Ⓑ 마케팅부 김진수 부장님 보러 왔습니다.
marketing dept. manager Kim Jinsu to see came
I came to see Mr. Kim Jinsu in Marketing.

- 외부인은 사무실 출입이 금지됩니다.
  outsider office access prohibited
  Non-employees are not allowed in the office.

- 방문증을 끊어 오세요.
  visiting ticket please get and come
  Please get a visitor's pass.

- 어느 부서에 볼일이 있으신가요?
  at which department business there be
  Which department are you here to visit?

○ **출입증을 안 가져왔어요.**

entrance ticket not brought

I didn't bring my pass/key card.

○ **택배 온 거 없었어요?**

door-to-door delivery come thing there not be

Did any packages arrive?

○ **택배 오면 좀 받아 주세요.**

door-to-door delivery come please take

If a package arrives, please sign for it.

A **여기 3층인데요. 잡상인이 돌아다니고 있어요.**

here 3rd floor be solicitor going around

This is the 3rd floor. There is a solicitor dup here.

B **바로 올라가겠습니다.**

right away will go up

I'll be right up.

○ **5층 복도에 이상한 사람이 있는데 좀 와 주세요.**

in 5th floor hallway strange person there be please come

There is a suspicious looking person in the 5th floor hallway. Can you please come up?

○ **여자 화장실에 이상한 사람이 있어요.**

at woman bathroom strange person there be

There is a strange person in the woman's bathroom.

○ **비상구 문이 잠겨 있습니다.**

emergency exit door locked

The emergency exit is locked.

Deliveries 06

In Korea, home delivery service providers can get you a book the very next day just about anywhere in the country. The price usually varies more according to volume than weight.

Ⓐ 네, 한림택배입니다.
yes Hollym Home Delivery Service be
Hello, this is Hollym Home Delivery Service.

Ⓑ 택배 보낼 게 있는데요.
door-to-door delivery to send there be
I have something to send.

퀵서비스 보낼 게 있는데요.
quick service thing to send there be
I have something to send by "quick service."

Ⓐ 어떤 물건입니까?
what kind thing be
What is it?

Ⓑ 서류봉투 하나예요.
document envelop one be
It's a document envelope.

지하철 퀵도 가능한가요?

subway quick possible

Can I also use the subway's quick service?

A 택배비가 얼마나 나올까요?

delivery charge how much come out

How much will delivery charges be?

B 배송 직원이 가서 확인해야 알 수 있습니다.

delivery staff should go verify can know

A delivery person will have to go check on the price.

박스 무게를 재 봐야 합니다.

box weight should measure

I have to weigh the box before I can say.

20킬로그램까지는 요금이 같습니다.
up to 20kg rate same
The price is the same up to 20kg.

박스 크기가 가로세로 얼마나 됩니까?
box size length and width how big
What is the length and width of the box?

A 택배비는 어떻게 계산하실 겁니까?
delivery charge how pay
How will you pay for delivery?

B 착불로 해 주세요.
later at arrival payment please
Please send it COD.

선불로 지불하겠습니다.
payment in advance will pay
I'll pay in advance.

보낼 물건하고 택배비는 경비실에 맡겨 놓겠습니다.
send goods delivery charge at security office will leave
I'll leave the item and the money at the security office.

A 받으시는 곳의 주소와 전화번호는 어떻게 됩니까?
receive place's address and telephone number what be
What is the address and phone number of the receiver?

B 서울 강남구 압구정2동 131-2 하나빌딩 3층 HR무역이고, 전화번호는 514-3512입니다.
Seoul Gangnam-gu Apgujeong 2-dong Hana Bldg. 3F. HR Trading company telephone number 514-3512 be
The address is HR Trading, 131-2 Hana Building 3rd Floor, Apgujeong 2-dong, Gangnam-gu, Seoul. The phone number is 514-3512.

보내시는 분의 주소를 말씀해 주세요.
send person's address please tell
Please tell me the sender's address.

받으시는 분의 주소를 말씀해 주세요.
receive person's address please tell
Please tell me the receiver's address.

A 언제쯤 도착할까요?
about when will arrive
About when will it arrive?

B 내일 오후에 도착할 겁니다.
tomorrow in afternoon will arrive
It should arrive tomorrow afternoon.

언제쯤 가지러 오실 건가요?
about when to pick up will come
About when will you come pick it up?

내일 오전에 기사가 고객님 댁을 방문할 겁니다.
tomorrow in morning driver customer's house will visit
A driver will visit your house sometime tomorrow morning.

물건은 경비실에 맡겨 놓겠습니다.
goods at security office will leave
I will leave it at the security office.

늦어도 모레 오후까지는 들어갈 겁니다.
at latest till the day after tomorrow afternoon will arrive
The latest it should arrive is the day after tomorrow afternoon.

모레 오전에 받아 보실 수 있을 겁니다.
in the day after tomorrow morning will get
You should get it by the day after tomorrow morning.

Caution

Do not put a business card in your pocket without first looking at it.

It is not polite to put a business card in your pocket without having first looked at it. And when giving your own card, always do so with the writing facing where your counterpart can read it.

Vocabulary

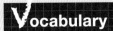

Office Furniture and Machines

책상
desk

의자
chair

컴퓨터 책상
computer desk

회의용 책상
conference table

회전의자
revolving chair

스탠드
lamp (desk lamp)

커피 테이블
coffee table

책장/책꽂이
bookcase/bookshelf

서랍
drawer

서랍장
drawers (chest)

파지 분쇄기 (파쇄기)
paper shredder

프린터
printer

스캐너
scanner

컴퓨터
computer

팩스
fax machine

복사기
copy machine

Stationery/Office Supplies

연필
pencil

샤프
mechanical (automatic) pencil

볼펜
ballpoint pen

네임펜
permanent pen

보드마카
board marker

형광펜
highlighter

지우개
eraser

수정액
correction liquid/correction pen

화이트/수정테이프
white-out

스테이플러
stapler

스테이플러 심
staple

가위
scissors

클립
clip

칼
knife

투명 파일
clear file

자
ruler

끈
cord/string

택배 봉투
delivery envelop

Inside the Company

사무실
office

리셉션/안내데스크
reception desk

사장실
president's office

구내식당
cafeteria

비서실
secretary's office

경비실
security office

회의실
meeting room

주차관리실
parking office

자료실
document room/reference library

창고
storage (warehouse)

탕비실
canteen

복도
hallway

휴게실
staff lounge

계단
stairway

흡연실
smoking room

비상구
exit

화장실
rest room

로비
lobby

1 Reporting Progress

2 Reporting Results

3 Reporting Market Research

4 Reporting on Rival Companies

5 Reporting Business Prospects

6 Presentations

7 Receiving Approval

8 Reports

CHAPTER 03

Reports

Reporting Progress 01

Ⓐ 얼마나 진행되었나요?
how much progressed
How far along are you?
How much progress have you made?

Ⓑ 제품 생산이 늦어지고 있는 상황입니다.
product production being delayed situation be
We are experiencing delays in production.

어디까지 진행되었습니까?
by where progressed
How far have you progressed?

얼마나 진행된 상황입니까?
how much progressed situation be
How much progress have you made?

시장 조사는 어떻게 돼 갑니까?
market research how being become
How is that market research coming?

현재 신제품에 대한 소비자 반응을 조사하고 있는 중입니다.
present about new product consumer response investigating
We are presently conducting research on consumer reactions to the new product.

대략 반 정도 진행됐습니다.

roughly around half progressed

We are about half done.

현재 적절한 론칭 시기와 론칭 방법을 구상하고 있습니다.

present proper launching time launching method conceiving

We are presently considering the ideal time and method for launching.

진행 상황은 파일로 첨부해서 보내겠습니다.

progress situation for file will attach and send

I'll send you my progress report as an attachment.

현장 조사를 마쳤습니다.

spot investigation done

We completed our on-site investigation.

A 혹시 진행 과정에 문제가 있습니까?

by any chance in progress process problem there be

Is there a problem with regard to progress?

B 제품 출시가 지연될 것 같습니다.

product release seem delayed

The product's release will likely be delayed.

진행 과정에 문제가 있는지 보고하세요.

in progress procedure problem there be please report

Please report whether there is a problem with regard to progress.

- **어떤 문제가 있습니까?**
  what kind problem there be
  What are the problems?

- **뭐가 문제입니까?**
  what problem be
  What is the problem?

- **진행 과정에서 변경된 사항이 있습니까?**
  in progress procedure changed fact there be
  Has anything changed with regard to progress?

- **별다른 문제는 없습니다.**
  peculiar problem there not be
  There are no real problems.

- **순조롭게 진행되고 있습니다.**
  smoothly being progressed
  Things are progressing smoothly.

- **예정대로 진행되고 있습니다.**
  as scheduled being progressed
  Things are progressing as expected.

- **차질 없이 진행되고 있습니다.**
  without miscarriage being progressed
  Things are progressing without any problems.

- **진행 일정에 대한 세부적인 검토가 필요합니다.**
  about progress schedule thorough inspection need
  We need a detailed evaluation of our scheduled progress.

- **계약 조건에 대해 재검토할 필요가 있는 것 같습니다.**
  about contract condition reexamination seem need
  I believe we need to reexamine the conditions of the contract.

거래처 담당 직원이 휴가라서 아직 확인을 못 하고 있습니다.
client's staff in charge on vacation yet confirm cannot
I am still unable to confirm because the person in charge is on vacation.

어떤 게 최종안인지 모르겠네요.
which one final plan not know
I don't know which is the final plan.

A 시간을 맞출 자신 있습니까?
time fit confidence there be
Are you confident you can do it on time?

B 네, 일정에 차질이 없도록 하겠습니다.
yes in schedule miscarriage there not be will do
Yes. I will make sure there are no deviations from the schedule.

시간 내에 다 될까요?
within time all will done
Will it be finished on time?

일정에 차질이 없겠지요?
in schedule miscarriage there would not be
There will be no deviations from the schedule, right?

예정보다 늦어지고 있습니다.
than schedule becoming late
We are falling behind schedule.

기한 내에 마무리할 수 있을 것 같습니다.

within due can seem finish

I believe we can finish it within the allotted time.

시간을 지킬 수 있을 것 같습니다.

time can seem keep

I believe we will be able to do it on time.

제작업체로부터 초안을 이메일로 받았습니다.

from manufacturer first draft revision by email got

I received a draft by email from the manufacturer.

전화로 초안 수정을 부탁드렸습니다.

by phone first draft requested

I called and requested a correction of the draft.

오늘 아침에 거래처에 데이터를 보냈습니다.
today in morning to client data sent
I sent the data to the client this morning.

내년 3월까지 제품을 출시하기로 했습니다.
next year by March product release supposed
We decided to launch the product by March of next year.

Hierarchical Relationships within an Organization

Many people have referred to Korea as a patriarchical and authoritarian society. Authoritarian is one way to describe the distinctly hierarchical nature of many Korean personal relationships. The relationships within the family, where people are expected to obey their parents, translate into a tendency to respect and obey superiors at work. Of course, when a difference of opinion exists, it can be extremely difficult for someone in a lower position to express his or her opinion.

Reporting Results 02

The period for reporting business results differs according to industry. Reports may be made daily, weekly, monthly, quarterly, or annually. In the transportation industry, reports are sometimes even made hourly.

A 이번 달 영업 실적 보고하세요.
this month sales record please report
Please report on this month's business results.
Please report on this month's sales.

B 지난 해 1/4분기와 비교할 때, 영업 실적이 약 15% 떨어졌습니다.
with last year first quarter compare sales record about 15% fell
Sales fell about 15% compared to the same quarter last year.

이번 분기 영업 실적 나왔습니까?
this quarter sales record came out
Has the performance report for this month come out?

이번 달 영업 실적은 어떻습니까?
this month sales record how
How were sales this month?

○ **이번 분기 영업 실적을 보고 드리겠습니다.**

this quarter sales record will report

I will give you report on sales for this quarter.

○ **판매량이 13.5% 증가했습니다.**

sales volume 13.5% increased

Sales increased by 13.5%.

○ **2010년 3월 중국 영업이 본격화된 이래 하반기 영업 실적이 20% 향상되었습니다.**

2010 year March China sales since fully activated the second half of the year sales record 20% improved

After fully activating business in China in March of 2010, the second half business performance improved by 20%.

○ **인건비 절감으로 인해 이익이 전 분기 대비 7.8% 증가했습니다.**

because of labor costs reduction profits contrast to previous quarter 7.8% increased

Due to reductions in the cost of labor, profits increased by 7.8% when compared to the previous quarter.

- **2010년 상반기 매출에 있어서 경쟁사에 비해 월등한 성과를 보였습니다.**

  2010 in terms of the first part of the year sales comparing rival company conspicuous achievement shown

  In terms of sales for the first half of 2010, we showed superior results when compared to rival companies.

- **전달 대비 5% 감소했습니다.**

  compare to previous month 5% decreased

  There was a 5% reduction compared to last month.

- **전 분기 대비 매출이 10% 떨어졌습니다.**

  compare to previous quarter sales 10% fell

  Sales fell 10% compared to the previous quarter.

- **사상 최대 실적을 기록했습니다.**

  in history greatest result recorded

  We recorded the best results in history.

- **6월부터 연속 감소해 11월에 가장 부진한 실적을 기록했습니다.**

  from June consecutively decrease in November most depressed result recorded

  Due to continuous reductions since June, we recorded our worst results ever in November.

- **실적이 개선될 여지가 있습니다.**

  record improve room there be

  There is room for improvement in our results.

Reporting Market Research 03

In general, reports begin with their conclusions. This is often what superiors want to hear first, followed by the reasons and processes behind those conclusions.

A **5분 후에 시장 조사 결과 보고하세요.**
five minutes later market research result please report
Please give us a report on the results of your market research in five minutes.

B **네, 바로 준비하겠습니다.**
yes right away will prepare
Alright. I'll prepare it now.

시장 조사 결과가 나왔습니까?
market research result came out
Have the results of our market research come out?

시장 조사 결과는 어떻습니까?
market research result how
How are the results of our market research?

제품 개발 전략을 세우기 전에 시장 조사부터 하도록 하세요.
product developing strategy before building from market research please do
You should carry out market research before establishing a strategy for product development.

- 소비자 만족도 조사를 실시한 결과는 다음과 같습니다.

  consumer satisfaction survey perform result as following

  The results of our research into degree of customer satisfaction are as follows.

- 이번 제품은 남성들에게도 어필하는 것으로 나타났습니다.

  this time product to men appeal turn out

  It turns out that the present product also appeals to men.

- 이번 제품의 구매층은 20-30대 여성들로, 작고 가벼우면서도 심플한 디자인을 선호하는 것으로 나타났습니다.

  this time product purchasing class 20-30s women small light simple design prefer turn out

  The present product is targeted at women in their 20s and 30s, who, it turns out, prefer small, light, and simple designs.

A **시장 조사 결과에 대한 의견을 개진해 보세요.**
about market research result idea please set forth
Please give us your opinion on the market research results.

B **타겟층을 좀 더 명확히 할 필요가 있는 것 같습니다.**
target class a little more clearly set seem need
I think we need to be a bit clearer about our target audience.

소비자의 구매 성향을 이해하려면, 문화적인 요인까지 분석해야 합니다.
consumer's purchase disposition to understand cultural cause should analyze
In order to understand the purchasing patterns of consumers, we need to analyze cultural factors as well.

소비자의 구매 행위를 분석해서 유통 경로를 설정해야 합니다.
consumer's purchase behavior analyze distribution channel should set up
We have to set up distribution channels after we have analyzed consumers' purchasing behavior.

Reporting on Rival Companies 04

A 경쟁사에 대해 조사한 것 보고하도록 하세요.
about rival company investigated thing please report
Please give us a report of your research on our rival company(ies).

B 이번 신제품은 경쟁사와 유사하기 때문에 제품 광고를 먼저 하는 것이 시급합니다.
this time new product with rival company similar product advertising in advance doing urgent
Because this new product is similar to that of our rival company(ies), it is imperative that we begin advertising first.

경쟁사에 대한 조사 결과가 나왔습니까?
about rival company investigation result came out
Have the results of our research on our rival companies come out?

요즘 경쟁사 동향은 어떻습니까?
recently rival company trends how
What our rivals are doing these days?

경쟁사 동향이 어떤지 좀 알아보도록 하세요.
rival company trends how please investigate
Please look into what our rivals are doing.

최대한 빠른 시일 안에 경쟁사의 동향을 파악하겠습니다.
within maximum fast days rival company's trend will figure out
I will figure out our rivals' actions as soon as possible.

A 요즘 SM사 동향은 어떤지 알아 봤습니까?
recently SM Company trends how investigated
Have you looked into what SM Company is doing these days?

B 금년 안에 대만 시장에 진출하려는 것으로 보입니다.
in this year to Taiwan market enter into seem
It appears as if they are planning to enter the Taiwanese market within the year.

경쟁사가 이번에 미국 HH의 플로리다 건설 건을 수주했다고 합니다.
rival company this time the US HH's Florida construction case obtained said
I heard that our rival won the bid for the HH construction deal in Florida.

- SM사가 이번에 미국 HH 트레이딩과 계약을 체결했다고 합니다.
  SM Company this time with the US HH Trading made contract said
  SM Company said they recently signed a contract with the US firm HH Trading.

- 만약 이번에 경쟁사가 먼저 베트남 시장에 진입한다면, 저희는 갈수록 어려워질 것입니다.
  if this time rival company first into Vietnam market enter we as time goes by will become difficult
  If our rival enters the Vietnamese market before us, things will grow increasingly difficult.

- 이번에 HH사가 어떻게 대응할지 모르겠습니다.
  this time HH Company how respond not know
  We have no idea how HH Company will respond this time.

- 이번 홈페이지 비방글은 조사 결과 경쟁사의 소행이었습니다.
  this time homepage slandering writing investigation result rival's conduct be
  Our research shows that the recent negative comments on our Website were actually posted by a rival company.

- 경쟁사에서 이번에 출시한 핸드폰은 주로 20대 여성에게 반응이 좋다고 합니다.
  rival company this time released cellular phone mainly to women in 20s response good said
  Our rival's most recent entry into the cell phone market is said to be getting a good response from women in their 20s.

Reporting Business Prospects 05

Monthly results are generally compared to those of the same month during the previous year, and from such comparisons, future business prospects are analyzed.

A **영업 전망이 어떤지 보고하세요.**
sales prospect how please report
Please give us a report on our business prospects.

B **연말에 환율이 올라갈 경우에 수익성이 5% 정도 향상될 것으로 내다보고 있습니다.**
at year-end exchange rate in case go up profit around 5% improve foresee
If exchange rates rise at the end of the year, we are predicting an increase in profits of approximately 5%.

영업 전망 분석한 것에 대해 보고하도록 하세요.
about sales prospect analyzed thing please report
Please give us a report on your analysis of business prospects.

영업 전망 분석 결과가 나왔습니까?
sales prospect analyzing result came out
Have the results of the analysis of business prospects come out?

판매율이 5% 증가할 것으로 예상됩니다.
sales rate 5% increase prospected
A 5% increase in the rate of sales is predicted.

신제품 출시로 내년 영업 전망이 밝습니다.

for new product release next year sales prospect bright

Next year's business prospects are bright thanks to the release of our new product(s).

신제품 자체 개발과 해외 진출로 장기 영업 전망이 밝습니다.

with new product self development and abroad entering long-term sales prospect bright

Thanks to our new product development and entrance into overseas markets, long-term business prospects are bright.

생산 시스템의 효율성 향상이 인건비를 절감시켜 수익성 개선에 기여할 것으로 예상됩니다.

producing system efficiency improvement labor cost reduce to profit betterment contribute expected

Improvements in the efficiency of the production system are expected to reduce labor costs and thereby contribute to improved profitability.

- 식료품은 작년 대비 판매율이 저조할 것으로 예상하고 있습니다.

  grocery last year compared sale rate dull forecasting

  We are predicting a slow rate of sales compared to last year for food products.

- 경기 침체에 따라 우리 회사의 영업 실적은 작년 대비 5% 정도 떨어질 전망입니다.

  economy depression according to our company's sales record last year compared around 5% fall prospect

  Due to a slow economy, it is expected that our company's profits will fall about 5% compared to last year.

- 내년 1/4분기까지 수익성 회복 전망이 불투명합니다.

  next year untill first quarter profit recovery prospect unclear

  Prospects for recovering profitability are murky through the first quarter of next year.

- 경쟁사와의 치열한 경쟁이 예측됩니다.

  with rival company keen competition predicted

  Fierce competition with our rival company(ies) is predicted.

Presentations 06

Korean companies have a tendency to value formal presentations. PowerPoint program is often used, but additional materials are also prepared for every aspect of the presentation and handed out to all participants.

- **오늘 발표를 맡게 된 중남미 마케팅 담당 김민준입니다.**
  today presentation take on Central and South America marketing in charge Kim Minjun be
  I am Kim Minjun, in charge of Central and South America Marketing, and I will be giving today's presentation.

- **그럼 프레젠테이션을 시작하겠습니다.**
  then presentation will start
  I will now begin my presentation.

- **먼저 프로젝트의 목적에 대해 설명하겠습니다.**
  first about project's goal will explain
  I will first explain the goals of this project.

- **준비한 자료를 보면서 말씀 드리겠습니다.**
  prepared data see will tell
  I will speak to you while viewing the materials I have prepared.

- **다음은 사진 자료들을 보시겠습니다.**
  following photo data will see
  Please look at the following photos.

이해를 돕기 위해 동영상을 준비했습니다.
understanding to help video prepared
I prepared a video to make it easier to understand.

지금 보시는 그래프는 경쟁사의 지난 해 영업 실적입니다.
now seeing graph rival company's last year sales record be
The graph you are now viewing shows our rival's performance for last year.

지금 보시는 것은 경쟁사에서 개발한 제품 사진입니다.
now seeing thing at rival company developed product picture be
What you are seeing now is a photo of a product developed by our rival company.

다음은 예상되는 문제점들입니다.
following expected problems be
The following are the expected problems.

지금까지 발표를 들어 주셔서 감사합니다.
untill now presentation listen thank you
Thank you for your attention.

이상으로 신제품 출시에 대한 프레젠테이션을 마치겠습니다.

for this about new product release presentation will finish

This concludes my presentation on the launch of our new product(s).

질문이 있으시면 언제든지 말씀해 주십시오.

question there be any time please tell

Please let me know if you have any question.

Caution

Do not use only one hand when receiving something from a superior.

Always use both hands when giving something to or receiving something from a superior. Using only one hand is considered very impolite.

Receiving Approval 07

Ⓐ **쇼핑몰 운영 계획입니다. 검토해 주십시오.**
shopping mall managing plan be please review
This is the plan for running the shopping mall. Please look it over.

Ⓑ **어디 봅시다.**
let's see
Let me see.

확인해 주십시오.
please confirm
Please check this out.
Please confirm this.

검토 바랍니다. review want
Please review.

재가 바랍니다. approval want
Please approve.

확인 바랍니다. confirmation want
Please confirm.

* The above three are used in writing, not speaking.

A **5월 2일부터 5월 7일까지 협력업체 방문 건으로 중국에 출장 갈 예정이니 보고 및 품의할 것이 있으면 그 기간은 피하도록 하세요.**

from May 2nd to May 7th for partner firms visit case China business trip plan to go if reporting and consulting thing there be the period please avoid

Since we are planning a trip to China to visit our partner company from May 2nd to May 7th, please avoid scheduling any reports or consultations during that period.

B **네, 그렇게 하겠습니다.**

yes so will do

Alright. I'll do that.

제가 부재 시에 김진수 부장이 업무를 대행할 예정이니 김 부장에게 보고하도록 하세요.

I absence in case manager Kim Jinsu duty execute expected to manager Kim please report

Since Mr. Kim Jinsu will fill in for me during my absence, please report to him.

출장 가시기 전에 품의서를 올리도록 하겠습니다.

business trip before go request for approval will submit

I will be sure to submit my request for approval before you leave for your business trip.

출장 다녀오신 후에 운영계획서를 올리겠습니다.

business trip after get back operations plan will submit

I will submit my operations plan after you return from your business trip.

Reports 08

Reports can be seen as a very important task because they are part of what helps those in charge decide whether or not to begin and continue certain projects. Most companies have their own individual formats for reports.

A **이번 달 말일까지 연차보고서를 작성하세요.**
by this month end annual report please write
Please complete the annual report by the end of this month.

B **네, 알겠습니다.**
yes understood
Alright./Okay./Understood.

다음 주까지 사업제안서를 써 오세요.
by next week business proposal please write and come
Please write up a business proposal by next week.

출장보고서 아직도 안 냈습니까?
business trip report yet not submitted
Have you still not submitted your business trip report?

기일 내로 제출하겠습니다.
within due date will submit
I will turn it in by the deadline.

A **보고서 제출 기한이 언제예요?**
report submit deadline when be
When is the deadline for submitting the report?

B **오늘 오후까지 출장보고서를 제출해야 됩니다.**
today by afternoon business trip report should turn in
You must submit a business trip report by this afternoon.

보고서 제출 기한을 연장해 주시면 안 될까요?
report submit deadline extend not allowed
Could you extend the report deadline?

시간이 너무 촉박합니다.
time too urgent
We are pressed for time.
There is not enough time.

- 아직 출장보고서를 작성 못 했습니다.
  yet business trip report not wrote
  I still haven't completed my business trip report.

- 다 작성했습니다.
  all wrote
  I'm all finished.
  I completed it.

A 이렇게 대충대충 작성하면 안 됩니다.
like this roughly write not allowed
You shouldn't give a lick and a promise to draw up a business report.

B 죄송합니다. 보완하도록 하겠습니다.
sorry make up will do
I am sorry. I will make the necessary additions.

- 좀 더 꼼꼼하게 작성해 보세요.
  more meticulously please write
  Please write it again more carefully.

- 다시 검토해 보고 보고하세요.
  again please review and report
  Please reinvestigate and then report.

- 좀 더 세밀하게 써 오세요.
  more minutely please write and come
  Please write it again with more details.

이건 좀 말이 안 되는 것 같은데요.
this a bit make not sense
This doesn't seem to make any sense.

틀에 맞게 해야지요.
to format right should do
You have to follow the proper format.

수정해서 내일 다시 보여 드리겠습니다.
modify tomorrow again will show
I will correct it and show it to you again tomorrow.

내일까지 수정하겠습니다.
by tomorrow will modify
I will correct it by tomorrow.

A 분기별 보고서를 어떻게 써야 할지 전혀 감이 안 와요.
quarterly report how write have no clue
I have no idea of what to do with the quarterly report.
I have no clue as to how to write the quarterly report.

B 작년 걸 참고해서 작성해 보세요.
last year one please refer and write
Refer to the report of the last year.

보고서 초안을 검토해 주시겠습니까?
report first draft will review
Please go over the first draft of the report.

◌ 이거 부장님께 제출할 건데 대리님께서 한번 읽어 봐 주시겠습니까?

this to manager submit supervisor once will read

I have to submit this to the manager, will you please look it over for me?

◌ 이거 제가 쓴 보고서인데 한국어가 괜찮은지 한번 봐 줄래요?

this I wrote report Korean okay once will review

I wrote this report. Would you please check if the Korean is okay?

◌ 방향을 보다 명확히 해야겠네요.

direction more clearly should set

You need clearer direction.

Vocabulary

Types of Forms

휴직계
request for time off from work

휴가계
leave request

시말서
written apology

사유서
letter of explanation

경위서
detailed report

사고 경위서
accident report

출장계
request for business trip

지각계
report of tardiness

결근계
report of absence

조퇴계
request for early leave

외출계
request for going out

명예퇴직신청서
application for early retirement

사표
letter of resignation

해고통지서
dismissal notice

인수인계서
transition report

기획안
project proposal

재직증명서
proof of employment

퇴직증명서
certificate of retirement

Reports

판매보고서
sales report

연차보고서
annual report

분기별 보고서
quarterly report

사업제안서
business proposal

시장조사 보고서
market research report

출장보고서
business trip report

비용 보고서
expense report

지출내역 보고서
expenditure report

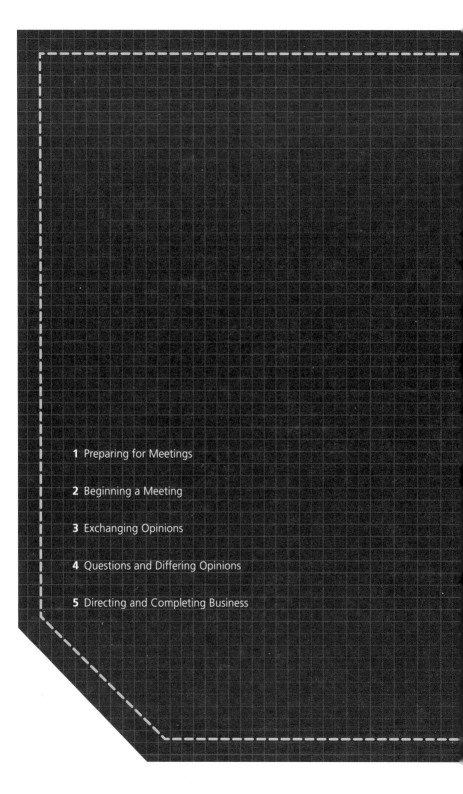

1 Preparing for Meetings

2 Beginning a Meeting

3 Exchanging Opinions

4 Questions and Differing Opinions

5 Directing and Completing Business

CHAPTER 04

Meetings

Preparing for Meetings 01

There are both regularly scheduled meetings to report on general progress and results, and occasional meetings called for particular matters. Various preparations, including notifying participants and reserving space, are required for successful meetings.

A 김 대리, 회의실 예약했습니까?

supervisor Kim meeting room reservation made

Ms./Mr. Kim, did you reserve a meeting room?

B 네, 2층 소회의실로 예약해 뒀습니다.

yes 2nd floor for small meeting room reservation made

Yes, I reserved the small meeting room on the 2nd floor.

- 이번 주간 회의는 사장님 출장 때문에 수요일로 미뤄졌습니다.

  this weekly meeting becasue of president's business trip to Wednesday postponed

  This week's meeting has been postponed until next Wednesday due to the president's business trip.

- 직원들에게 알리고 스케줄 조정하도록 하세요.

  to employees notice schedule change

  Please tell the employees and change the schedule.

회의 시간과 장소를 문자 메시지로도 알리도록 하세요.

meeting time and place by text message please notice

Please send a text message regarding the time and place of the meeting.

회의실 예약은 인트라넷으로 해야 되지요?

meeting room reservation through Intranet should do

We have to reserve meeting rooms through the Intranet, right?

회의실을 예약하려면 인트라넷에 들어가서 회의 내용과 일정을 입력해서 승인을 받아야 됩니다.

meeting room to reserve into Intranet enter meeting content and schedule type in must get approval

If you want to reserve a meeting room, you have to get on the Intranet and enter the agenda and schedule for approval.

메일로 내용 전달하고 회의실 예약 재확인하도록 하겠습니다.

by email content deliver meeting room reservation will reconfirm

I will notify you by email and reconfirm the meeting room reservation.

Beginning a Meeting 02

Unlike presentations, which are often made by one designated person, meetings involve many people, and are most often run by the most senior person in attendance.

A **오늘 회의 안건이 뭐예요?**
today meeting agenda what be
What is the agenda for today's meeting?

B **오늘 안건은 신제품 홍보 행사에 대한 거예요.**
today agenda new product PR event be
Today's agenda involves publicity events for our new product(s).

- 모두 모이셨습니까?
  all gathered
  Is everyone here?

- 다 왔으면 이제 시작할까요?
  if all came now shall start
  If everyone's here, shall we begin?

- 회의를 시작하겠습니다.
  meeting will start
  Shall we begin the meeting?

- 회의에 앞서 MG와의 계약 체결에 대한 브리핑이 있겠습니다.
  prior to meeting about contract with MG briefing there will be
  Before we begin the meeting, there will be a briefing on the contract we signed with MG.

- 홈페이지 운영에 대한 새로운 의견이 있으시면 자유롭게 말씀해 주시기 바랍니다.
  about homepage operation new opinion if there be freely please tell
  If anyone has new ideas for the operation of our homepage, please speak freely.

- 누가 회의록을 작성할 거지요?
  who minutes will write
  Who will write up the minutes?

Exchanging Opinions 03

Ⓐ 새로운 아이디어가 있으면 말씀해 주십시오.
new idea if there be please tell
Please tell me if you have any new ideas.

Ⓑ 제가 생각하기에는 동남아 지역의 시장 규모가 얼마나 되는지 파악하는 것도 중요합니다.
I think Southeast Asian area market size how big figure out important
In my opinion, it is also important that we ascertain the scale of the market in the Southeast Asian region.

돌아가면서 한 사람씩 의견을 말해 보도록 하죠.
in turn one person each opinion let's state
Let's go around the room and have each person give his or her opinion.

새로운 트렌드에 맞춰 유연하게 변화하고 도전할 필요가 있습니다.
to new trend adjust flexibly change challenge need
We need to respond flexibly to new trends.

제 생각에는 20대 소비자 구매 성향을 재조사할 필요가 있는 것 같습니다.
in my thought 20s consumer purchase trend reinvestigate seem need
In my opinion, we need to reexamine the purchasing trends among consumers in their 20s.

제 생각을 말씀 드리면 현재 진행하고 있는 프로젝트는 전면적인 수정이 필요한 것 같습니다.

my idea if say current progressing project overall modification seem need

In my humble opinion, we need a total overhaul of the present project.

A 제가 먼저 얘기해도 될까요?

I first can say

May I speak first?

B 네, 말씀하십시오.

yes please speak

Yes, please do.

제 생각은 이렇습니다.

my idea like this

I believe the following.

제가 먼저 얘기하겠습니다.

I first will say

I will speak first.

그럼 제가 설명 드리겠습니다.

then I will explain

Well then, let me explain.

제가 보충 설명을 드려도 되겠습니까?

I supplementary explanation can give

May I provide some additional explanation?

박 부장님의 질문에 대해서 제가 답변해도 될까요?

about manager Park's question I can answer

May I answer Ms./Mr. Park's question?

A 3개월 안에 신제품을 출시하는 것은 무리인 것 같습니다.

within three months new product release seem hard

I don't think we will be able to release the new product within three months.

B 저도 같은 생각입니다.

I also same thought be

I feel the same way.

저도 김 과장님과 같은 의견인데요.

I also with manager Kim same opinion be

I agree with Ms./Mr. Kim.

전적으로 동의하는 바입니다.

totally agree

I completely agree.

저도 그 제안에 동의합니다.

I also to the suggestion agree

I agree with that suggestion.

Meeting Manners

When expressing opinions or asking questions during a meeting, it is important not to interrupt others. Always wait for a speaker to finish before asking a question, and be sure to speak clearly and in a controlled pace. Also try to make eye contact with others in the room in order to gauge their level of interest and understanding.

When seats are assigned and there is a designated presenter, the highest ranking person will usually be seated directly across from the presenter, and the other senior members will be seated to either side of the highest ranking person in descending order of seniority.

Questions and Differing Opinions 04

Ⓐ 질문이 있으시면 언제든지 편하게 말씀해 주십시오.

question if there be any time easily please say

If you have any questions, please feel free to ask at any time.

Ⓑ 조금 전에 신제품 출시 일정을 앞당길 수 있다고 하셨는데, 좀 더 구체적으로 설명해 주시겠습니까?

a little before new product release schedule move up said more concretely will explain

Earlier you said it would be possible to launch the new product early; could you please provide a more detailed explanation?

조금 전에 말씀하신 투자 계획이 이해가 되지 않습니다.

a little before said investment plan cannot understand

I don't understand the investment plan you mentioned earlier.

질문에 대해서 간단하게 답변 드리겠습니다.

about question simply will answer

I will give you a brief answer.

I will provide a simple explanation.

A **타이완 진출에 대해서는 재고해 볼 필요가 있습니다.**
about Taiwan entering need try to reconsider
We need to reconsider our entry into Taiwan.

B **저는 이 과장님과는 좀 다른 생각입니다.**
I with manager Lee a little different thought be
I have a slightly different opinion from Ms./Mr. Lee.

저는 김민호 씨의 의견에 반대합니다.
I to Mr. Kim Minho opinion oppose
I am opposed to Mr. Kim Minho's opinion.

SM사의 제안을 수락하기 어렵습니다.
SM Company's suggestion accept hard
SM Company's suggestion will be difficult to accept.

발상의 전환이 필요한 것 같습니다.
concept change seem need
I believe we need a change in our thinking.

박 부장님께서는 신제품 개발을 앞당기는 것이 좋겠다고 하셨는데 반드시 그런 것 같지는 않습니다.

manager Park new product development move up good said necessarily seem not so

Ms./Mr. Park said it would be good to speed up new product development, but I don't necessarily agree.

그런 면이 없지는 않지만 그렇지 않은 경우도 있는 것 같습니다.

such aspect there be but not like that case there seem be

That is true at times, but there are also cases in which it is not.

Caution

Do not refer to others using the word "당신."

Although the word "당신," meaning "you," is quite polite in written Korean, in spoken Korean, with very few exceptions, it is used as a somewhat pejorative version of the second person pronoun. When addressing one's superiors, it is appropriate to use their surname followed by the polite form of their official title: 김 부장님; 박 과장님; 이 대리님; etc. For those on an equal level to you, the polite "–님" suffix may be omitted: 김 부장; 박 과장; etc.

Directing and Completing Business 05

A **동남아 지역 시장 규모 분석은 김 대리가 맡아 주세요.**
Southeast Asian region market size analysis supervisor Kim please take
Ms./Mr. Kim, please take charge of analyzing the scale of the market in the Southeast Asian region.

B **네, 알겠습니다.**
yes understood
Alright. I'll do that.

기존 상품에 대한 마케팅 전략을 검토하는 일은 이 과장이 맡아 주시기 바랍니다.
about existing product marketing strategy examining work manager Lee please take
Ms./Mr. Lee, I want you to handle the examination of our marketing strategy for existing products.

김 과장은 오늘 회의 결과에 대한 구체적인 제안을 짜서 올리도록 하세요.
manager Kim about today meeting result specific suggestion please make and report
Ms./Mr. Kim, please come up with a concrete proposal regarding the results of today's meeting.

A 그럼 다른 의견이 없으면 오늘 회의는 이것으로 마치겠습니다.
then different opinion if there be not today meeting for this will finish
Well, if there are no objections, I will end today's meeting.

B 수고하셨습니다.
took effort
thank you for your trouble
Good job.
Thank you.

회의가 예상보다 좀 길어졌습니다.
meeting than expected a little lengthened
The meeting ran longer than planned.

더 하실 말씀 없으시면 이제 결론을 내려 볼까요?
more speech if there not be now conclusion shall make
If there are no further comments, shall we make a decision?

이쯤해서 마무리해 볼까요?
for now shall finish
Shall we wrap things up?

이것으로 오늘 회의를 마치겠습니다.
for this today meeting will finish
With that, I conclude today's meeting.

자, 모두들 수고하셨습니다.
well you all took effort
Well, everyone did a great job.
Well, you all worked very hard.

오늘 긴 회의에 끝까지 함께 해 주신 여러분께 감사 드립니다.
today long meeting till end together to you thank
Thanks to all of you for staying with me today through this long meeting.

A 오늘 결정된 사안은 회사 전체 메일로 회람시키도록 하세요.
today decided item company entire by email please send round
Please use email to circulate the items we decided upon today to the entire company.

B 네, 그렇게 하겠습니다.
yes so will do
Will do.

오늘 회의 내용은 김민호 씨가 정리해 두세요.
today meeting content Mr. Kim Minho please organize
Mr. Kim Minho, please organize the contents of today's meeting.

○ **작성한 회의록을 나한테 이메일로 보내세요.**

written minutes to me by email please send

Please send me the minutes by email.

○ **이번 회의에서 결정된 사안은 내일 전무님께 보고할 계획입니다.**

at this meeting decided item tomorrow to executive director plan to report

I plan on reporting the items decided upon in this meeting to the executive director tomorrow.

○ **오늘 회의에서 결정이 안 난 사안은 다음 회의에서 다시 다루도록 합시다.**

at today meeting decision not came out item at next meeting again let's handle

Let's deal with those items left undecided today in our next meeting.

Vocabulary

Terms for Meetings

개회 선언
calling the meeting to order

회의록
the minutes

미결
pendency

과반수
majority

다수결
majority vote

표결
vote

동의
assent

심의
deliberation

의결 사항
matters for decision

다수결의 원칙
the principle of majority voices

Departments

기획부
Planning department

영업부
Sales department

회계부
Finance department

인사부
Personnel/Human Resources

마케팅부
Marketing department

총무부
General Affairs department

구매부
Purchasing department

생산부
Production department

연구개발부
R&D department

설비관리부
Facilities Maintenance department

자재관리부
Materials Management department

품질관리부
Quality Control department

정보기술부/전산부
IT department

1 Making Calls

2 Receiving Calls

3 Leaving Messages

4 Taking Messages

5 Relaying Messages

6 Ending Calls

7 Bad Connections

CHAPTER 05

Business Telephone Calls

Making Calls 01

When making a telephone call to a company, you can reach a person by using the following: "name/title+계십니까?" or "name/title+좀 바꿔 주세요."

Ⓐ 한림상사입니다.
Hollym Trading be
Hollym Trading.

Ⓑ 마케팅부 김은정 부장님 부탁합니다.
marketing dept. manager Kim Eunjeong request
May I please speak with Ms. Kim Eunjeong in Marketing?

Ⓐ 잠깐만 기다리세요. 연결해 드리겠습니다.
for a minute please wait will connect
One moment, please. I'll connect you.

- 총무부 이 대리님 좀 바꿔 주시겠습니까?
General Affairs dept. supervisor Lee please would put on
May I please speak with Ms./Mr. Lee in General Affairs?

- 맥캔지 컨설팅의 존 리입니다. 박명수 부장님 계십니까?
McKenzie Consulting John Lee be manager Park Myeongsu there be
This is John Lee from McKenzie Consulting. Is Mr. Park Myeongsu in?

회계과 좀 연결해 주세요.
Accounting dept. please connect
Please connect me with the Accounting department.

과장님 자리로 전화 돌려 드리겠습니다.
to manager seat phone will put through
I will transfer your call to the manager.

내선번호 456번 부탁합니다.
extension 456 request
Extension 456, please.

A 거기 SM무역이죠? 영업 담당자와 통화를 하고 싶은데요.
there SM Trading be with sales person in charge would like to talk
This is SM Trading, right? I would like to speak to the person in charge of sales.

B 영업부로 전화 돌려 드리겠습니다.
to Sales dept. phone will put through
I will transfer your call to the Sales department.

문의드릴 게 있어서 전화했는데요.
thing to inquire there be called
I called because I have a question.

출장 일정에 대해 말씀 드릴 게 있어서 전화 드렸습니다.
about business trip schedule thing to tell called
I called because I have something to tell you about the business trip schedule.

A 김민호 씨 내선번호가 몇 번이지요?
Mr. Kim Minho extension what number be
What is Mr. Kim Minho's extension number?

B 김민호 씨는 내선번호 3427입니다.
Mr. Kim Minho extension 3427 be
Mr. Kim Minho's extension number is 3427.

- 회사 내에서 전화할 때는 어떻게 전화해요?
  inside company when call how call
  How do I make a call within the company?

- 내선번호와 샵 버튼을 누르세요.
  extension and sharp button please press
  Dial the extension and press the pound key.

- 별표 누르고 5636번 누르세요.
  star sign press number 5636 please press
  Press the star key and then dial 5636.

외부에 통화하실 때는 9번 누르고 전화 거시면 돼요.
to outside when call number nine can press and call
When calling outside you must first dial a 9.

A 김진수 씨 핸드폰입니까?
Mr. Kim Jinsu mobile phone be
Is this Mr. Kim Jinsu's cell phone?

B 네, 전데요. 실례지만 누구십니까?
yes me excuse (me) but who be
Yes, this is he. Excuse me, but who is this?

밤늦게 전화 드려 죄송합니다.
late at night called sorry
Sorry to be calling so late.

급한 일이라 핸드폰으로 전화를 드렸습니다.
urgent work to cellular phone called
It was urgent so I called you on your cell phone.

Receiving Calls 02

When receiving calls at work, you should first say the name of your company, then your department, followed by your name "○○사 ○○부 ○○○입니다." When the call comes from inside your own company, you may omit the company name "○○부 ○○○입니다."

A 네, HR상사 영업부 배용준입니다.
yes HR Trading sales division Bae Yongjun be
Hello, this is Bae Yongjun, Sales division, HR Trading.

B 배 대리님, 안녕하세요? 저는 IPM의 이준영입니다.
supervisor Bae how are you I IPM's Lee Junyeong be
Hello, Mr. Bae. This is Lee Junyeong from IPM.

이상준 과장님 계십니까?
manager Lee Sangjun there be
May I please speak with Mr. Lee Sangjun?

네, 배용준입니다.
Yes Bae Yongjun be
Hello, this is Bae Yongjun.

네, 전데요.
yes me
Yes, this is she/he.

잠깐만 기다리세요. 이 과장님 전화로 연결해 드리겠습니다.
for a minute please wait to manager Lee's phone will connect
One moment, please. I will connect you with Ms./Mr. Lee.

끊지 말고 기다리세요.
hang up not please wait
Please stay on the line.

경리부로 연결해 드리겠습니다.
to Accounting department will connect
I will connect you with the Accounting department.

혹시 끊어지면 2345로 다시 하시기 바랍니다.
by any chance disconnected to 2345 again please do
If we get disconnected, please call back at 2345.

A **이 과장님 계십니까?**
manager Lee there be
Is Ms./Mr. Lee in?

B **이 과장님 지금 자리에 안 계신데요.**
manager Lee now in seat there not be
Ms./Mr. Lee is not in at the moment.

김 과장님 외근 나가셨습니다.
manager Kim working away went out
Ms./Mr. Kim is out of the office today.

지금 회의 들어가셨습니다.
now meeting went in
She/He is in a meeting now.

죄송하지만 지금 회의 중이십니다.
sorry but now in meeting
I am sorry, but she/he is in a meeting right now.

김민호 씨는 지금 휴가 중입니다.
Mr. Kim Minho now on vacation
Mr. Kim Minho is on vacation.

이 과장님 지금 통화 중이십니다.
manager Lee now calling be
Ms./Mr. Lee is on another line at the moment.

A **언제쯤 돌아오십니까?**
about when come back
When is she/he due back?

B **핸드폰 번호를 가르쳐 드릴 테니 한번 연락해 보시겠어요?**
cellular phone number will teach once will contact
I'll give you her/his cell phone number. Why don't you try her/him there?

회의가 몇 시에 끝날까요?
meeting at what time will end
When will the meeting be over?

오늘 중으로 들어오실까요?
within today will come back
Will she/he be back in today?

김 이사님 핸드폰 번호 좀 알려 주시겠습니까?
director Kim cellular phone number please would inform
Could you please tell me Director Kim's cell phone number?

오후에 회사로 들어오실 겁니다.
in afternoon to company will come back
She/He will be back in the office this afternoon.

A 실례지만 어디십니까?
excuse (me) but where be
Excuse me, but with whom am I speaking?

B Kim & Lee 컨설팅의 이 전무라고 전해 주십시오.
Kim & Lee Consulting's executive director Lee please convey
Please tell her/him that Executive Director Lee from Kim & Lee Consulting called.

- 실례지만 누구십니까?
  excuse (me) but who be
  Excuse me, but who is this?

- 실례지만 전화하시는 분 성함이 어떻게 되십니까?
  excuse (me) but calling person name what be
  Pardon me, but may I have your name?

- 전화 받으시는 분 성함이 어떻게 되십니까?
  taking phone person name what be
  May I please have your name?

- 죄송하지만 무슨 일이십니까?
  sorry but what matter be
  I'm sorry, but why are you calling?

- 실례지만 무슨 일 때문에 그러십니까?
  excuse (me) but because of what matter do so
  Excuse me, but what seems to be the matter?

Writing Telephone Memos

When your company has pre-printed memo forms, it is best to use them. When these are not provided, you may use the examples below. It is best to end sentences with the formal "–(스)ㅂ니다" form, or to write in phrases ending with "–(으)ㅁ."

이 부장님,

HT 컨설팅 이수진 과장에게 전화 왔었습니다.
어제 보낸 이메일 확인하시고 답변 달라고 합니다.

5월 9일 3:20p.m.
김민호 드림

Dear Ms./Mr. Lee,

Ms. Lee Sujin from HT Consulting called.
She asked that you check the email she sent you yesterday and get back to her.

Kim Minho
May 9, 3:20p.m.

이준상 씨,

전화한 사람: IPM 마케팅부 김상혁 과장
내용: 9일에 보낸 사업계획서 검토 결과를 알고 싶음

9월 18일 2:10p.m.
박민수

To Mr. Lee Junsang,

Caller: Mr. Kim Sanghyeok from IPM's Marketing department
Message: Wants to know the results of your evaluation of the business plan he sent on the 9th

Park Minsu
September 18, 2:10p.m.

03 Leaving Messages

Ⓐ 메모 좀 전해 주시겠습니까?
memo please would hand in
Could you please give her/him a message?

Ⓑ 네, 말씀하세요.
yes please say
Yes, go ahead.

메시지 좀 남겨도 될까요?
message can leave
May I leave a message?

회의가 취소됐다고 전해 주세요.
meeting cancelled please convey
Please let her/him know that the meeting has been cancelled.

김 과장님 오시면 PT자료를 내일까지 이메일로 보내겠다고 전해 주십시오.
manager Kim when come presentation data by tomorrow through email will send please convey
When Ms./Mr. Kim comes in, please let her/him know that I will email the presentation materials by tomorrow.

나중에 다시 연락 드리겠습니다.
later again will contact
I'll call back later.

오늘 오후에 다시 연락 드리겠다고 전해 주십시오.
today in the afternoon again will contact please convey
Please tell her/him that I'll call back this afternoon.

편하실 때 전화 부탁 드린다고 전해 주세요.
at ease call request please convey
Please have him call me whenever it is convenient.

Taking Messages 04

A 메모 전해 드릴까요?
memo will hand in
Shall I give her/him a message?

B 네, 그렇게 해 주시면 좋겠습니다.
yes so if do will be good
Yes, that would be nice.

메시지 남기시면 전해 드리겠습니다.
message if leave will convey
If you leave a message, I'll make sure she/he gets it.

들어오시는 대로 메모 전하겠습니다.

as soon as come back will hand in

I'll give her/him your message as soon as she/he returns.

회의가 끝나는 대로 전화 드리도록 메모 전하겠습니다.

meeting as soon as end to call memo will hand in

I'll give her/him a message to call you as soon as the meeting is over.

연락처 남기시면 들어오시는 대로 연락 드리라고 말씀 드리겠습니다.

contact address if leave as soon as come back to contact will tell

If you leave me your phone number, I'll have her/him call you as soon as she/he comes in.

제가 내일 다시 전화 드리겠다고 전해 주십시오.

I tomorrow again will call please convey

Please tell her/him I'll call back tomorrow.

Making International Phone Calls

When calling overseas from Korea, you should use the following: "International Service Provider Number+Country Code+Phone Number." For example, if you wished to call the US number 617-713-4782, you could dial 001/002/00700 (Service Provider)+1 (Country Code)+6177134782 (Phone Number).

Relaying Messages 05

Ⓐ IPM의 홍보 담당자에게 전화 왔었습니다. 메모는 부장님 책상 위에 두었습니다.

IPM's PR person in charge call came memo manager on desk put

You received a call from the person in charge of publicity at IPM. I put a note on your desk.

Ⓑ 고마워요.

thank you

Thank you.

AG 김 부장님에게서 전화 왔었습니다.

from AG manager Kim call came

You received a call from Ms./Mr. Kim at AG.

들어오시면 전화해 달라고 하셨습니다.

when come back to call told

She/He told me to have you call when you come in.

30분 전에 한림무역 박 과장에게서 연락 왔었습니다.

30 minutes before Hollym Trading manager Park contact came

Ms./Mr. Park from Hollym Trading called 30 minutes ago.

포스트잇에 메모해서 컴퓨터 모니터에 붙여 뒀습니다.

on Post-it memo on computer monitor attached

I put a Post-it note on your computer monitor.

Caution

Don't hang up before a superior.

When you are speaking with a superior on the phone, you should wait until he or she has hung up before you end your call.

06 Ending Calls

When ending a phone call, you may use "안녕히 계세요." —just as you would in person—or use more specific phrases such as "네, 잘 알았습니다." or "그럼 연락 기다리겠습니다." which are appropriate to the specific situation and denote that the conversation has been finished. If the call was to make an appointment, saying something to reconfirm such as "네, 그럼 토요일 강남역에서 두 시에 뵙겠습니다." is a good way to conclude.

A **안녕히 계세요.**
well please be
Good-bye.

B **네, 들어가세요.**
yes please go in
Good-bye.

네, 알겠습니다.
yes understood
Understood.
Yes, I'll make sure to do that.

네, 감사합니다.
yes thank
Yes. Thank you.

그럼 잘 부탁 드립니다.

then well request

Well then, thank you very much.

연락 기다리겠습니다.

contact will wait

I'll await your call.
I hope to hear from you soon.

네, 그럼 그때 뵙겠습니다.

yes well then will meet

Okay. Well, I'll see you then.

네, 수고하십시오.

yes take effort

Okay. Good-bye.

Bad Connections 07

When you get disconnected, it is customary for the person who made the call to call back. When the person who made the call is a superior, however, you should immediately call him or her back.

A 네? 뭐라고 하셨습니까? 9시라고 하셨습니까?
yes what said nine o'clock said
Yes? What was that you said? Did you say 9 a.m.?

B 네, 회의는 내일 9시니까 시간 지키세요.
yes meeting tomorrow by nine o'clock please keep time
Yes. The meeting is tomorrow at 9 a.m., so please be there on time.

잘 안 들립니다.
well not hear
I can't hear you.

전화 감이 좀 멀어요.
call reception distant
It sounds like you're far away.

전화가 지직거립니다.
call fizzing
There is a bunch of white noise.

네? 내일 회의가 취소됐다고요?
pardon tomorrow meeting cancelled
Yes? Did you say tomorrow's meeting was cancelled?

죄송하지만 좀 크게 말해 주실 수 있으세요?
sorry but a little loudly can say
I'm sorry, but can you speak a bit louder?

전화 상태가 좋지 않습니다. 좀 더 큰소리로 말씀해 주시겠습니까?
call condition not good a little more with louder voice would say
This connection is not very good. Could you please speak a bit louder?

A 주변에 영어하는 분 계시면 좀 바꿔 주시겠습니까?
around English speaking person if there be please put on
If there is someone who speaks English, could you please put him on?

B 잠깐만 기다리세요.
for a moment please wait
One moment, please.

영어로 다시 말씀해 주시겠습니까?
in English again would say
Would you please say that again in English?

죄송하지만 좀 천천히 말해 주실 수 있으세요?
sorry but a little slowly could speak
I'm sorry, but could you speak a bit more slowly?

죄송하지만 좀 빨리 말해 주실 수 있으세요?

sorry but a little fast could speak

I'm sorry, but could you speak a bit faster?

A 지금 배터리가 얼마 없어서 전화가 끊어질 수도 있습니다.

now battery much there not be call might disconnected

The battery is running low, so we may get cut off.

B 끊어지면 제가 나중에 다시 전화 드리겠습니다.

if disconnected I later again will call

If we get disconnected, I'll call back later.

지금 엘리베이터 안이라서 전화가 끊어질 수도 있습니다.

now inside elevator call might disconnected

I'm in the elevator now, so we may get disconnected.

손님, 죄송합니다. 전화가 잠시 끊겼습니다.

customer sorry call for a moment cut off

Ma'am/Sir, I apologize. We got disconnected.

Vocabulary

Types of Phones and Calls

무선전화/휴대전화
cell phone

유선전화
wire telephone/land line

전화 요금
telephone bill

시외전화
long distance call

시내전화
local call

국제전화
international call

공중전화
public phone

Country and Area Codes

Country Codes

대한민국 Republic of Korea 82
미국 USA 1
일본 Japan 81
중국 China 86
대만 Taiwan 886
러시아 Russia 7
캐나다 Canada 1
영국 UK 44
호주 Australia 61
프랑스 France 33
브라질 Brazil 55
홍콩 Hong Kong 852

Area Codes

서울 Seoul 02
인천 Incheon 032
대전 Daejeon 042
부산 Busan 051
울산 Ulsan 052
대구 Daegu 053
광주 Gwangju 062
제주 Jeju 064
경기 Gyeonggi 031
강원 Gangwon 033
충남 Chungnam 041
충북 Chungbuk 043
경북 Gyeongbuk 054
경남 Gyeongnam 055
전남 Jeonnam 061
전북 Jeonbuk 063

1 Computers

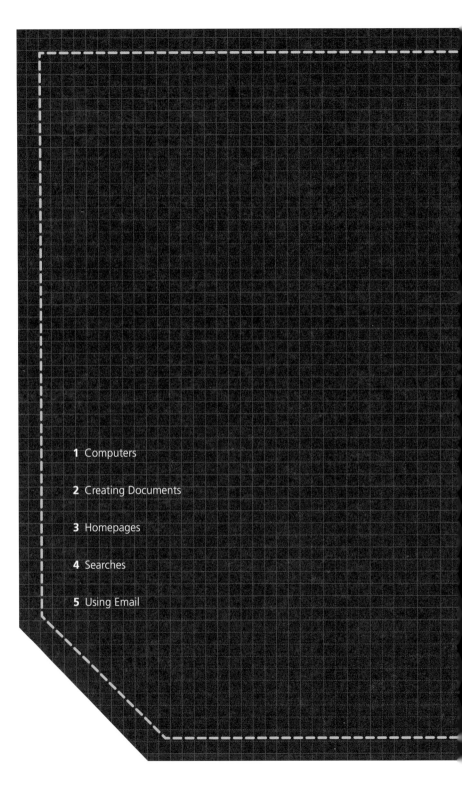

2 Creating Documents

3 Homepages

4 Searches

5 Using Email

CHAPTER 06

Computers and the Internet

Computers 01

The Korean government conducts regular and spot checks to make sure that people are not using illegal or pirated software. Under no circumstances should any unlicensed software be installed on a company computer.

A **제 컴퓨터가 바이러스에 걸린 것 같아요.**
my computer to virus seem to get
I think my computer has a virus.

B **백신 프로그램을 사용하면 해결할 수 있어요.**
vaccine program if use can solve
You can get rid of it with a vaccine program.

겨우 완성했는데, 파일이 날아가 버렸어요.
hardly completed file lost
I was almost finished when my file got erased.

부팅이 안 됩니다.
booting not possible
It won't boot up.

김 과장님 컴퓨터에 이상이 있는 것 같습니다.
manager Kim computer abnormal seem
Ms./Mr. Kim's computer seems to have a problem.

한글이 안 쳐져요.
hangeul not typed
I can't type in Korean.

파일이 안 열립니다.
file not open
The file won't open.

모니터가 너무 흐릿하게 보입니다.
monitor too blurry look
The monitor is too fuzzy.

한글이 깨져서 보입니다.
hangeul broken seen
The Korean letters come out jumbled.

인터넷이 안 돼요.
Internet not possible
The Internet isn't working.

이 노트북 무선 인터넷 돼요?
this laptop wireless Internet possible
Can I get wireless Internet on this notebook?

컴퓨터 메모리가 부족한지 속도가 너무 느립니다.

computer memory insufficient speed too slow

Perhaps this computer doesn't have enough memory; it is really slow.

제가 원격으로 문제를 파악할 동안 마우스를 움직이지 말고 기다려 주세요.

I by remote while problem grasp mouse not move please wait

While I am figuring out the problem by remote, please don't move the mouse.

서버 역할을 하는 컴퓨터는 전원을 끄지 마세요.

server role doing computer switch not turn off

Please don't turn off the server computer.

사내 모든 컴퓨터는 네트워크를 공유하고 있습니다.

within the company all computer network sharing

All computers in the company share a network.

사무실 컴퓨터는 모두 네트워크로 연결돼 있습니다.

office computer all with network connected

All computers in the office are connected to the network.

보안에 문제가 없도록 조심하세요.

to security problem there be not please be careful

Please be careful to avoid security problems.

Korea's High-Speed Internet

Korea is one of the best places in the world for nearly universal access to high-speed Internet. This was made possible by thoroughgoing government support and a relatively small land mass to cover. Of course, the Korean culture of "빨리빨리"—a national demand for speed in all things—also played a part.

Creating Documents 02

The two most common word processing programs in Korea are MS Word and Hangeul. Government agencies and schools tend to use Hangeul, while most companies use MS Word.

Ⓐ 버전이 달라서 파일이 안 열리는 것 같아요.
version different file not open seem
I think the file won't open because the version is different.

Ⓑ 제가 한번 해 볼게요.
I once will try do
Let me give it a try.

이 컴퓨터에 파워포인트 설치돼 있어요?
in this computer PowerPoint installed
Is PowerPoint installed on this computer?

한글 프로그램으로 작성하지 말고, MS 워드로 작성하세요.
with Hangeul program not make with MS Word please make
Please don't use Hangeul to compose this document; use MS Word.

간단한 통계는 엑셀로도 가능합니다.
simple statistics also with Excel possible
For simple statistics, Excel works fine.

우리 부서에서 누가 엑셀을 잘해요?

in our department who Excel do well

Who in our department is good at Excel?

파일명을 제출자 이름으로 해 주세요.

file name sender name please set

Please set the composer's name as the file name.

편집 양식이 안 맞네요.

editing form at not right

This is not the right editing format.

이 부분은 제가 작성한 파일에서 복사해서 붙이면 되겠어요.

this part I made from file can copy and paste

You can copy and paste this part from the file I made.

이번 달 영업 실적 분석 자료는 부장님이 주신 파일에서 잘라서 붙였습니다.

this month sales record analysis data manager gave from file cut and pasted

I cut and pasted this month's sales record report from the file you gave me.

Homepages 03

For security reasons and to boost productivity, many companies limit Internet acess, particularly to things such as random searching, buying and selling stocks, and chatting. When this happens, you must use the company's Intranet blog or proprietary search database.

A 오늘 회사 홈페이지에 우리 부서 사람들 사진을 올렸어요.
today at company homepage our department people picture uploaded
A photo of the people in our department is on the company homepage today.

B 그래요? 한번 가 봐야겠네요.
so once should go
Really? I should check it out.

오늘 회사 홈페이지 방문자 수가 1,000명을 넘었습니다.
today company homepage visitor number 1,000 exceeded
Today over 1,000 people visited our company's Website.

홈페이지 게시판 관리자가 누구지요?
homepage board administer who be
Who is the message board administer on this Website?

A 한림무역 홈페이지 주소 좀 알려 주세요.
Hollym Trading homepage address let me know
Will you let me know Hollym Trading's Website address?

B 저희 회사 홈페이지 주소는 www.hollym.co.kr입니다.
our company homepage address www.hollym.co.kr be
Our company's Website address is www.hollym.co.kr.

어제 홈페이지 방문자가 너무 많아서 홈페이지가 다운됐었습니다.
yesterday homepage visitor too many homepage went down
Our homepage crashed yesterday from too many visitors.

ID를 발급받아야 합니다.
ID issue should get
You must be issued an ID.

비밀번호를 주기적으로 변경하는 게 좋습니다.

password regularly change good

It is good to change your password periodically.

해킹 당했습니다.

hacking suffered

I got hacked.

제 홈페이지에 글 남겨 주세요.

at my homepage writing please leave

Please leave a comment on my homepage.

Caution

Don't begin eating before a superior.

When you are eating with a superior, you should wait for him or her to pick up a spoon or chopsticks (that is, to begin eating) before you do.

Searches 04

There are many people who blindly believe all the information available through Web portal sites, but you should always be careful since just about anything can be posted on the Internet.

○ **포털 사이트에 들어가서 검색해 보세요.**

in portal site please go and search

Please do a search at a portal site.

○ **지식 검색에서 찾아보세요.**

from knowledge search please find

Please look it up on the Web.

○ **인터넷 지식 검색에 나와 있던데요.**
at Internet knowledge search reported
I saw it on the Internet.

○ **인터넷 검색으로 찾은 거예요.**
by Internet search found
I found it on the Internet.

○ **포털 사이트 실시간 검색어 순위에 들었습니다.**
portal site real-time search word in ranking
It was ranked on the portal's real-time survey results.

○ **지금 실시간 검색어 순위 1위가 올림픽이네요.**
now real-time search word ranking first place Olympic be
The Olympics are currently ranked number one on the real-time search results.

○ **검색해 봤는데 인터넷에는 안 나와 있네요.**
searched on Internet not appeared
I searched for it, but it's not on the Internet.

○ **인터넷에서 인물 검색해 보면 그 사람에 대한 정보가 나올 거예요.**
on Internet person if search about the person information will appear
If you search on the Internet, you'll get information on that person.

○ **그런 정보는 사내 DB에 많이 있어요.**
those information in internal DB a lot there be
There's a lot of such information on the company's database.

Using Email 05

그분의 이메일 주소를 모르겠습니다.
her/his email address would not know
I don't know her/his email address.

메일을 보낼 때 수신 확인으로 보내세요.
when email send receive confirmation please send
When you send an email, request delivery confirmation.

그 메일은 보낸 메일함에 있을 거예요.
the email in sent mail box there may be
That message should be in your sent folder.

이메일을 보냈는데 되돌아왔습니다.
email sent but returned
I sent email but it was returned.

메일함 용량이 부족한 것 같습니다.
mailbox capacity insufficient seem
You don't seem to have enough space in your mailbox.

○ **파일 첨부가 안 되어 있습니다.**
file attachment not be
There is no file attached.

○ **파일 용량이 너무 커서 이메일로 보낼 수가 없네요.**
file size too big by email cannot send
The file is too large to be sent by email.

○ **웹하드에 올려 주세요.**
on Web-hard please upload
Please put it on Web-hard drive.

○ **파일을 첨부 안 하고 보내셨습니다. 다시 보내 주세요.**
file not attached sent again please send
You sent it without attaching the file. Please resend it.

○ **이메일 주소 좀 알려 주십시오.**
email address please let know
Please tell me your email address.

○ **이 주소는 업무용 이메일 주소입니다.**
this address for business email address be
This is my business email address.

○ **이메일로 연락하시면 됩니다.**
by email can contact
You can contact me by email.

○ **명함에 제 이메일 주소가 나와 있습니다.**
on business card my email address appear
My email address is on my business card.

○ **홈페이지에 나와 있는 주소로 보내 주세요.**
homepage appeared to address please send
Please send it to the address on our homepage.

Vocabulary

Computers

켜다
turn on

끄다
turn off

저장하다
save

복사하다
copy

삭제하다
delete

프로그램을 설치하다
install a program

클릭하다
click

다운되다
to go down/to break down

바이러스
virus

백신
vaccine

대용량 파일
large volume file

웹하드
Web-hard drive

동영상
moving picture/video

이미지 파일
image file

마이크
microphone

보안시스템
security system

화상회의
video conference

부팅시키다
boot up (the computer)

Emoticons

^^
smile

*^^*
blushing

ㅜ_ㅜ/-.ㅜ/ㅠㅠ
sadness

^^;
perplexed

--;/-_-
sweating

@.@
dizziness

./^.~
wink

Internet

검색하다
to search

검색어
search keyword

관련검색어
related search keyword

채팅하다
to chat

메신저
messenger

홈페이지/홈피
homepage

파일을 올리다/업로드하다
to upload (a file)

다운로드하다/다운받다/내려받다
to download (a file)

창
window

검색창
search window

수신자/받는 사람
receiver

발신자/보내는 사람
sender

전달자
messenger

냉무 (내용무)
no content

해킹
hacking

해커
hacker

계정
account

아이디
ID

비밀번호/패스워드
password

웹캠
Web camera

첨부하다
to attach

용량
capacity (storage capacity)

로그인하다
to log in

로그아웃하다
to log out

회원 가입하다
to sign up (for membership)

회원 탈퇴하다
to cancel/withdraw
(one's membership)

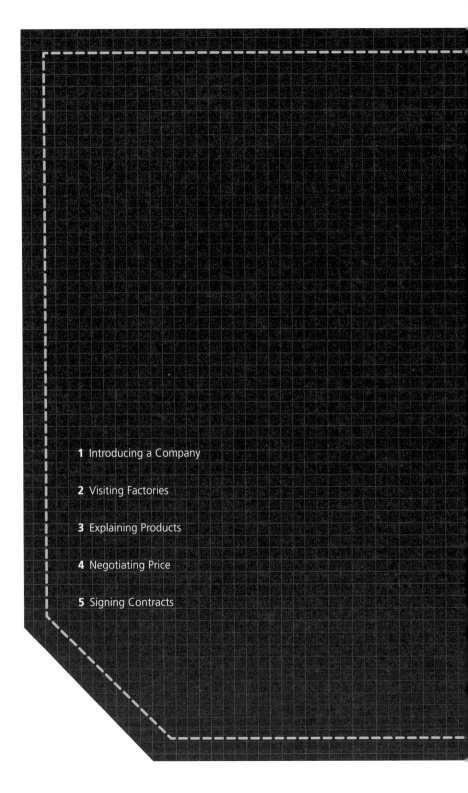

1 Introducing a Company

2 Visiting Factories

3 Explaining Products

4 Negotiating Price

5 Signing Contracts

CHAPTER 07

Negotiations and Contracts

Introducing a Company 01

Detailed descriptions of companies are often given to investors when trying to attract new investments, but when people visit a company a brief introduction is usually sufficient. In the latter case, things such as the main areas of business, number of employees, amount of sales, and growth trends are normally mentioned.

Ⓐ 간략하게 회사 소개를 좀 해 주시겠습니까?

briefly company introduction please would do

Would you please give us a brief introduction of your company?

Ⓑ 저희 회사는 가습기 생산 전문업체입니다. 연간 매출량이 200억에 달하는 국내 최대 가습기 생산업체입니다.

our company humidifier production professional company be annual sales 20 billion reach domestic largest humidifier production company be

Our company specializes in producing humidifiers. We do about 20 billion won in sales per year, making us the largest domestic manufacturer of humidifiers.

연간 100만 달러의 정부 지원을 받고 있습니다.

annual one million dollars government aid getting

We are receiving one million dollars in government support per year.

- 현재 아시아 5개국에 진출해 있습니다.
  currently Asia into five countries entered
  We are currently operating in five major Asian countries.

- 3년 연속 100대 유망 중소기업에 들었습니다.
  three years consecutively top 100 promising small and medium enterprises listed
  We have been among the top 100 small and medium sized companies for the past three years running.

- 우리 회사는 작년에 연간 수출이 300만 달러를 넘었습니다.
  our company last year yearly export three million dollars exceeded
  Our company surpassed three million dollars in annual exports last year.
  Our company's annual exports exceeded three million dollars last year.

- 저희 회사는 재무 구조가 탄탄하기로 유명합니다.
  our company financial structure healthy famous
  Our company is famous for its healthy financial structure.

Ⓐ **회사 규모는 어떻습니까?**

company size how

How large is your company?
What is the scale of your company?

Ⓑ **지난 해 총 6개의 신규 점포를 추가적으로 오픈해 현재 전국적으로 총 17개의 지점을 갖추고 있습니다.**

last year total six new stores additionally open currently nationally total 17 branch offices have

Last year we opened a total of six new stores, and we presently have a total of 17 stores nationwide.

○ **저희 회사 고객으로는 SD전자와 AG건설 등이 있습니다.**

our company for client SD Electronics and AG Construction etc. there be

Among our company's clients are SD Electronics and AG Construction.

○ **동남아시아에서의 시장점유율을 확대할 계획입니다.**

in Southeast Asia market share plan expand

We plan to expand our market share in Southeast Asia.

○ **고객의 앞선 생활문화를 선도하는 고품격 유통 그룹이 되고자 노력하고 있습니다.**

customer's life culture leading high quality distributing group to become making effort

We are working hard to become a high-quality distribution group that leads in improving the cultural lives of our customers.

- **저희 회사는 아동복지를 비롯한 다양한 사회 공헌 활동을 전개하고 있습니다.**
  our company child welfare including various society contribution activity developing
  Our company is involved in child welfare and various other activities that make a social contribution.

- **최근 10년간 양적인 성장과 더불어 질적으로도 성장을 하였습니다.**
  during recent 10 years with quantitative growth qualitatively also grown
  Over the last ten years, we have seen continued growth in both quantity and quality.

- **업계 최초로 2년 보증 서비스를 실시하는 등 고객에게 보다 다양한 상품과 서비스를 제공하고 있습니다.**
  industry field for the first time two-year guarantee service perform to customer more various product and service providing
  We were the first in the field to offer two-year warranties, and are always endeavoring to provide more diverse products and services to our customers.

- **차별화된 서비스를 제공하고 있습니다.**
  differentiated service providing
  We provide differentiated services.
  We provide unique services.

Visiting Factories 02

오늘 본사를 방문하신 것을 환영합니다.
today headquarters visiting welcome
Today welcome you to our headquarters.

즐겁고 유익한 방문이 되시기 바랍니다.
pleasant and profitable visiting please become
I hope you have a pleasant and rewarding visit.

Ⓐ 이 공장의 직원은 몇 명쯤 됩니까?
this factory's employee about how many people be
About how many people work at this factory?

Ⓑ 현재 750명이 2교대로 근무하고 있습니다.
present 750 people by two shift working
We presently have 750 people working in two shifts.

생산라인의 50%가 자동으로 가동되고 있습니다.
production line's 50% automatically being operated
50% of our production line is automated.

1995년부터 생산라인 자동화로 대량생산이 가능해졌습니다.
from 1995 production line thanks to automation mass production became possible
From 1995, with the automation of our production line, large scale production became possible.

국내 최대 규모입니다.

domestic greatest size be

It's the largest in the country.

5단계 공정을 거쳐 제품이 완성됩니다.

five level process pass product completed

Products are completed through a five-step process.

신기술 개발로 생산비 15%를 절감하고 있습니다.

new technology thanks to development production cost 15% reducing

We are reducing production costs by 15% by developing new technology.

생산 시설 규모가 국내 최대입니다.

production facilities scale domestic largest be

We have the largest production facilities in the country.

A 일일 생산량이 어떻게 됩니까?

daily production output how be

How many do you produce per day?

B 일일 생산량은 40대입니다.

daily production output 40 pieces be

Daily production is 40 pieces.
We produce 40 pieces per day.

- **연간 15,000대를 생산하고 있습니다.**

  annually 15,000 pieces producing

  We are producing 15,000 pieces per year.

- **전체 생산공정의 자동화를 계획 중에 있습니다.**

  entire production process automation planning

  We are planning to automate all production processes.

Explaining Products 03

Ⓐ 이 모델이 올해 신제품입니까?
this model this year new product be
Is this model one of this year's new products?

Ⓑ 아니요, 그 모델은 작년에 나온 겁니다.
no the model in last year came out
No. That model came out last year.

이 제품은 어떤 특징이 있습니까?
this product what characteristic there be
What is special about this product?

저희 회사 제품은 품질이 아주 우수합니다.
our company product quality very excellent
Our company's products have excellent quality.

이 제품은 국내 최초로 개발된 제품입니다.
this product domestic first developed product be
This product was the first of its kind to be developed domestically.

고객 반응이 좋은 제품입니다.
customer response good product be
This product is receiving good responses from customers.

요즘 가장 잘 팔리는 제품입니다.
recently best selling product be
This product is currently our best seller.

이 제품은 아직은 인지도가 높지 않습니다.
this product yet awareness not high
This product is still not very well known.

A 제품의 성능은 어떻습니까?
product's performance how
How is the product's performance?

B 작년에 국가에서 보장하는 품질인증을 받았습니다.
in last year nation guarantee quality certification received
Last year we received a guarantee of quality issued by the government.

저희는 하청업체에 맡기지 않고 자체 생산하고 있습니다.
we to subcontractor not assign own producing
We do not use subcontractors, but produce everything ourselves.

출고 전에 반드시 성능 테스트 과정을 거치고 있습니다.
before release certainly performance test procedure going through
They are all undergoing performance testing before being released.

본사에서는 무엇보다 품질 향상을 위해 주력하고 있습니다.
head office most of all for quality improvement concentrating
At headquarters, more than anything else, we are putting our efforts into improving quality.

유명 브랜드의 부품을 사용하여 신뢰할 수 있습니다.
famous brand's accessory use can trust
We use parts from famous brand makers so you can trust them.

Ⓐ 다른 제품들과 차별화되는 부분은 어떤 것입니까?
with other products differentiated part what be
What differentiates it from other products?

Ⓑ 저희 회사 제품은 보증기간이 3년인데, 보증기간 내 무상으로 수리를 해 드리고 있습니다.
our company product guarantee term three year during guarantee term for free fixing
Our products have a three-year warranty, during which we make all repairs free of charge.

반품률이 상당히 낮은 편입니다.
return rate considerably sort of low
We have a considerably low rate of returns.

시장점유율이 가장 높은 편입니다.
market share sort of most high
It has the highest market share.

Negotiating Price 04

A **생각보다 비싸네요.**
than expected expensive
It's more expensive than I expected.

B **이 정도면 싸게 사시는 겁니다.**
if this degree cheap buy
At this price you're buying it really cheap.

생각보다 가격이 세네요.
than expected price expensive
It costs more than I expected.

얼마를 원하십니까?
how much want
How much would you like to pay for this?

이 정도면 좋은 조건입니다.
if this degree good condition be
This is a pretty good deal.

더 싸게 드리고 싶지만, 이게 최저 가격입니다.
more cheap want to give this lowest price be
I would like to give it to you cheaper, but this is as low as I can go.

죄송하지만, 더 이상은 불가능합니다.
sorry but more not possible
I'm sorry, but any more is not possible.

Ⓐ **좀 더 싸게 안 될까요?**

a little more cheap not possible

Couldn't you make it just a little bit less?

Ⓑ **죄송하지만, 저 혼자 결정할 수 있는 일이 아닙니다.**

sorry but I alone can decide matter not be

I'm sorry, but this is not something I can decide by myself.

절충의 여지가 있습니까?

compromise room there be

Is there room for compromise?

사장님과 상의해 보겠습니다.

with boss will try consult

I will consult with the president.

윗분과 얘기해 보고 말씀 드려야겠습니다.
with senior will talk and say
I will speak with my supervisor and get back to you.

Ⓐ 얼마까지 할인해 주실 수 있는지 궁금하네요.
by how much can discount wonder
I'm wondering how much you can discount it.

Ⓑ 이번 주 안에 계약하시면 10% 할인해 드릴 수 있습니다.
within this week make contract 10% can discount
If you sign a contract within this week, I can give you a 10% discount.

작년에 출시된 제품은 할인해 드릴 수 있습니다.
in last year released product can discount
I can give you a discount on last year's products.

100대 이상 대량 주문하시면 할인해 드릴 수 있습니다.
more than 100 pieces bulk order can discount
If you order over 100 pieces, I can give you a discount.

정가에서 10% 빼드릴 수 있습니다.
from list price 10% can discount
I can take 10% off the normal price.

A 판매 계약 조건은 어떻게 됩니까?
sales contract condition how
What are the conditions of the sales contract?

B 계약금으로 10%를 미리 내셔야 합니다.
for earnest money 10% in advance should submit
You have to put 10% down to sign the contract.

지불 조건이 어떻게 됩니까?
payment condition how
What are the conditions for payment?

6개월 분할 납부하셔도 됩니다.
six month by installment can pay
You may pay it in installments over six months.

지불 기한은 3월 31일까지입니다.
payment deadline March 31st by be
Payment must be made by March 31st.

송장 발급일로부터 30일 이내에 지불해 주십시오.
from invoice issue date within 30 days please pay
You must make payment within 30 days of the invoice being issued.

FOB 방식으로 처리하는 게 좋겠습니다.
by FOB way managing would be good
I would like to do this FOB.

CIF로 계약합시다.
for CIF let's contract
Let's make a CIF contract.

A **현금으로 지불하면 좀 더 할인이 가능합니까?**
by cash if pay a little more discount possible
If I pay in cash, can I get a bit more of a discount?

B **네, 현금으로 하시면 10% 할인해 드립니다.**
yes by cash if do 10% discount
Yes. If you pay in cash, we'll give you a 10% discount.

지불은 어떻게 하실 건가요?
payment how will do
How would you like to pay?

내일까지 신용장을 개설하겠습니다.
by tomorrow a letter of credit will open
I'll open a letter of credit by tomorrow.

The Korean Preference for Indirectness

Even when rejecting an offer or proposal, Koreans will often avoid such negative statements as "안돼요," "싫어요," and "아니요." Because direct refusal may hurt a counterpart's feelings, indirect statements such as "하고 싶지만, 다른 일 때문에 도저히 시간을 낼 수가 없네요." will more often be used.

Signing Contracts 05

Larger companies will often hire a law firm or use an in-house legal team when signing contracts.

A 계약 기간이 2년 맞지요?
contract term two year right
The contract term is two years, correct?

B 네, 2년 맞습니다.
yes two years right
Yes, two years is correct.

계약서에 자세히 명시돼 있습니다.
in contract in detail clearly stated
It is clearly specified in the contract.

계약서 문구는 양사가 합의한 대로 작성했습니다.
contract phrase two companies as agreed wrote
I wrote up the contract as agreed upon by both companies.

오늘은 가계약 하시고, 다음 주에 정식으로 계약을 하시면 됩니다.
today make provisional contract next week formally can contract
Today we will sign a provisional contract, and next week we can sign the actual contract.

○ **계약 기간은 2년입니다.**

contract term two years be

The term of the contract is two years.

A **계약 위반 사항에 대해서 한 번 더 확인해 보십시오.**

about contract violation item once more please confirm

Please check one last time the items that constitute a breach of contract.

B **여기에 서명하면 되지요?**

here can sign

I can sign here, right?

○ **이제 서명만 하시면 됩니다.**

now only sign do

Now all you have to do is sign.

여기에 서명하시면 됩니다.

here sign do

You may sign here.

계약 당일로부터 법적인 효력이 발생됩니다.

from contract the day legal effect come into force

The contract is legally binding from the day it is signed.

특약에 추가하고 싶으신 부분이 있으면 지금 말씀해 주십시오.

special contract want to add part if there be now please tell

If there is something you would like to add to the special contract, please tell us now.

Caution

Do not use only one hand when shaking hands with a superior.

When shaking hands with a superior, it is impolite to use only one hand. You should either hold or support your right hand with your left, and then shake hands using your right.

Korean Curreney

There are no personal checks in Korea, but when you need to pay large sums you may use bank cheques. Paper bills include 50,000, 10,000, 5,000, and 1,000 won notes while there are 500, 100, 50, and 10 won coins.

Bills

1,000 won		Yi Hwang (1501-1570) Joseon Dynasty Confucian scholar
5,000 won		Yi Yi (1536-1584) Joseon Dynasty Confucian scholar
10,000 won		King Sejong the Great (1418-1450) 4th Monarch of the Joseon Dynasty, inventor of hangeul
50,000 won		Shin Saimdang (1504-1551) Joseon Dynasty literary woman, a model of wise mother

Coins

10 won		Dabotap Pagoda
50 won		Rice stalks
100 won		Yi Sunshin (1545-1598) Famous Joseon Dynasty admiral
500 won		Crane

Vocabulary

Trade

FOB (Free On Board) 본선인도가격

CIF (Cost, Insurance & Freight) 운임보험료포함조건

CNF (Cost & Freight) 운임포함조건

DDU (Delivered Duty Unpaid) 관세미지급인도조건

DDP (Delivered Duty Paid) 관세지급인도조건

B/L (Bill of Lading) 선하증권

C/O (Certificate of Origin) 원산지 증명서

CY (Container Yard) 컨테이너 야적장

P&I (Club Protection & Indemnity Club) 선주책임상호보험

UCP (Uniform Customs and Practice for Commercial Documentary Credits) 신용장통일규칙

INCOTERMS (International Rules for the Interpretation of Trade Terms) 무역조건 해석에 대한 국제규칙

T/T (Telegraphic Transfer) 전신환

D/A (Document against Acceptance) 환어음 인수도조건

D/O (Delivery Order) 인도지시서

CAD (Cash Against Delivery) 선적서류상환불

COD (Cash On Delivery) 현금결제

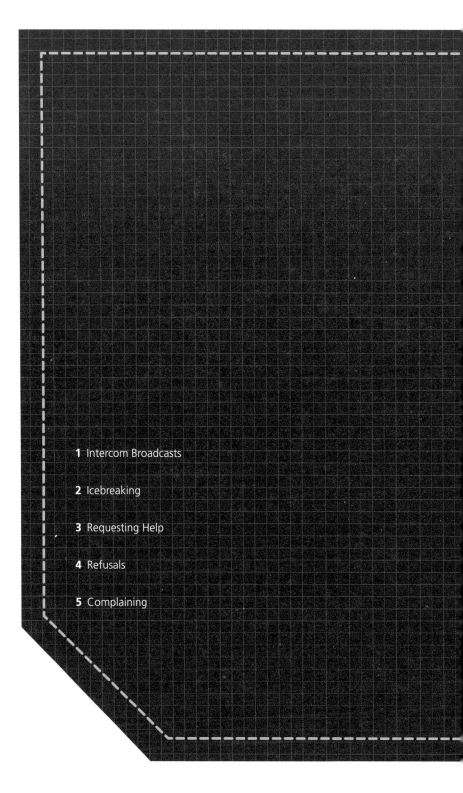

1 Intercom Broadcasts

2 Icebreaking

3 Requesting Help

4 Refusals

5 Complaining

CHAPTER 08

Office Interactions

Intercom Broadcasts 01

4월 17일부터 사내 교육이 실시될 예정이오니, 희망자는 12일까지 신청해 주시기 바랍니다.

from April 17th internal training planned held person who want by 12th please apply

The company will be conducting education from April 17th; all those interested should apply by the 12th.

이번 주 금요일에 세미나가 있으니, 참석 대상자는 참석하시기 바랍니다.

this week on Friday seminar there be attend person please attend

There is a seminar this Friday, so we hope all relevant personnel will attend.

이번에 500만 달러 프로젝트를 수주하게 되었습니다. 애써 주신 임직원 여러분께 감사 드립니다.

this time five million dollars project order get served employees appreciate

We recently received an order for a five-million-dollar project. Thank you to all the employees involved.

Icebreaking 02

Talking about the weather or asking whether someone has eaten yet are customary ways of breaking the ice. Asking about meals works well since it implies a concern for the other person's welfare.

Ⓐ 오늘 날씨 참 좋죠?
today weather very good
Nice weather today, isn't it?

Ⓑ 네, 날씨가 많이 풀렸어요.
yes weather very much got warm
Yes, it has warmed up quite a bit.

식사하셨어요?
meal had
Have you eaten?

헤어스타일 바뀌셨네요.
hair style changed
I see you have a new hair style.

부장님, 이발하셨어요?
manager got hair cut
Did you get a haircut?

넥타이가 잘 어울리십니다.
tie very go well
That tie looks good on you.

파란색이 참 잘 어울리시네요.
blue color very much go well
Blue looks really good on you.

오늘 무슨 좋은 일 있으세요?
today what kind good thing there be
Is today a special occasion?

요즘 뭐 안 좋은 일 있으세요?
these day what not good thing there be
Is something the matter these days?

Requesting Help 03

Ⓐ 연차보고서 이렇게 쓰는 것 맞나요?
yearly report like this write right
Is this the right way to write an annual report?

Ⓑ 한번 봅시다. 여기를 좀 고쳐야겠네요.
once let me look here a little should fix
Let me have a look. You'll have to fix this part.

사업제안서는 어떻게 작성하죠?
business proposal how make
How do you write a business proposal?

이거 이렇게 하는 거 맞아요?
this like this do right
Is this the right way to do it?

엑셀 사용해서 자료 정리하는 법 좀 가르쳐 주세요.
Excel by using material arrange method please teach
Can you please teach me how to use Excel to organize this data?

한번 써 보세요. 나중에 제가 한번 봐 줄게요.
once try write later I once will review
Just write it first. I'll have a look at it later.

A **이거 인사부에 좀 갖다 주세요.**
this to HR please take
Please take this over to HR.

B **네, 지금 바로 전달하겠습니다.**
yes right now will convey
Yes, I'll deliver it right away.

위층에 가는 길에 홍보부에 이 서류 좀 갖다 주세요.
upper floor go on the way to PR this document please take
On your way up, will you please take these forms to PR?

오늘 중으로 작년 시장 조사 보고서 찾아서 내 책상 위에 올려놓으세요.
within today last year market research report find on my desk put
Please find the last year's market research report and have it on my desk by the end of the day.

이거 일본어로 번역해 오세요.
this into Japanese please translate and come
Please translate this into Japanese.

A 도와주면 뭐 해 줄 거예요?
if help what will do
If I help you, what will you do for me in return?

B 나중에 밥 살게요.
later meal will buy
I'll buy you a meal later.

이거 해 주면 나한테 뭐 해 줄 거예요?
this if do to me what will do
If I do this, what's in it for me?

도와주면 나중에 한턱 낼게요.
if help later will treat
If you help me, I'll buy a lunch/dinner sometime.

도와줄 테니까 나중에 한잔 사세요.
will help later buy drink
I'll help you, so buy me a drink later on.

Korean Vacations and Vacation Spots

Jejudo Island is the most popular vacation destination inside Korea. It has an exotic feel and weather is pleasant enough during all four seasons. During the summer, the coastal areas and rivers are popular, while the ski resorts of Gangwon-do Province attract visitors during the winter.

Refusals 04

It is very difficult, if not impossible, to refuse an order or request from superiors or seniors. When a colleague or junior asks for a favor, however, it is perfectly permissible to refuse or defer.

A **김민호 씨, 이것 좀 도와줄래요?**
Mr. Kim Minho this please will help
Mr. Kim Minho, will you please help me with this?

B **지금 좀 급한 일이 있어서 그러는데, 이따가 도와드리면 안 되겠습니까?**
now a little urgent business there be later if help not possible
I actually have some really urgent business right now. Could I help you later?

○ **잠깐만요. 5분 후에 가겠습니다.**
for a minute five minutes later will go
One moment. I'll be there in five minutes.

○ **일이 많아서 지금은 정신이 하나도 없어요.**
work a lot now out of mind
I'm really swamped right now.

○ **지금 좀 바쁜데요. 나중에 하면 안 될까요?**
now a little busy later do can do
I'm kind of busy right now. Can't it wait?

○ **이런 건 저보다는 김 대리가 잘 알 거예요. 김 대리에게 물어 보시는 것이 좋을 것 같습니다.**
this kind than me supervisor Kim well will know to supervisor Kim try to ask seem good
Ms./Mr. Kim will know more about this matter than I do. You should probably ask her/him.

○ **부장님이 부르셔서 가 봐야 하니 이따가 도와줄게요.**
manager call should go later will help
The manager called me so I have to go, but I will help you later.

○ **못 도와줘서 미안해요. 내 코가 석 자예요.**
can't help sorry my nose ninety centimeter be
I'm sorry I can't help you. I'm absolutely swamped.

Caution

Don't wave to elders or superiors.

In Korea, when greeting an elder or superior, you should always bow. Waving is considered rude.

Complaining 05

○ **할 일이 태산 같아요.**
work to do like mountain
I have mountains of work to do.

○ **요새 눈코 뜰 사이 없어요.**
nowadays eyes and nose open time there not be
These days I'm incredibly busy.

○ **바빠 죽겠어요.**
busy would be dead
I'm deathly busy.

○ **일에 눌려 살아요.**
by work pressed live
I have piles of work pressing down on me.

○ **해도 해도 끝이 없네요.**
do and do end not there be
No matter how much I do, it never ends.

○ **발등에 불이 떨어졌어요.**
top of the foot fire fell
I have no time to spare.

○ **아, 맨날 야근이야.**
ah everyday overtime work be
Geez, I'm working nights all the time.

주말에도 출근해야 돼요.
even weekend should go to work
I have to go in to work on the weekends.

우리 회사는 퇴근시간이 없어요.
our company closing hour there not be
At our company we never get off work.

A 보고서 쓰는 게 지긋지긋하네요.
report writing tired of
I'm sick and tired of writing reports.

B 저도 다음 주까지 끝내야 하는 보고서가 세 개나 있어요.
I also by next week should finish report even three there be
I also have three reports to finish by next week.

이번 일은 진짜 힘들어요.
this work really hard
This newest assignment is really hard.

하기 싫어 죽겠어요.
to do hate to death
I really hate doing this.

당장 때려치우고 싶어요.
right away want to quit
I want to quit right now.

- **이 일은 정말 적성에 안 맞네요.**
  this work really to aptitude not suit
  This work really doesn't suit me.

- **사표 쓰고 싶어요.**
  resignation letter want to write
  I want to tender my resignation.

- **정말 못 하겠어요.**
  really cannot do
  I really can't do this.

- **하기 싫으면 관두세요.**
  if hate quit please
  If you hate it so much, just quit.

- **박 부장님은 왜 나만 미워해요?**
  manager Park why only me hate
  Why does Ms./Mr. Park only pick on me?

Korean Holidays: 빨간날

National holidays, Sundays, and other official holidays are marked in red on calendars, and so commonly referred to as "빨간날," or "red days."

Vocabulary

Occupations

회사원
office worker

의사
doctor

간호사
nurse

사업가
businessman

변호사
lawyer

판사
judge

검사
investigator

승무원
flight attendant

컴퓨터 프로그래머
computer programmer

패션 디자이너
fashion designer

인테리어 디자이너
interior designer

미용사/헤어 디자이너
hair dresser/hair designer

건축가
architect

군인
soldier

외교관
diplomat

교사/선생님
teacher

교수
professor

강사
instructor/lecturer

연구원
researcher

목사
pastor

스님
Buddhist monk

운동선수
athlete

연예인
entertainer

비서
secretary

판매원/영업사원
sales person

보험판매원
insurance sales person

1 Waiting on Customers

2 Serving Refreshments

3 Dealing with Orders

4 Order Changes, Exchanges, and Refunds

5 Delivery Delays · Payment Problems

6 Warranties and After Service

CHAPTER 09

Customer Service

Waiting on Customers 01

Ⓐ 판매 책임자 좀 만나러 왔습니다.
sales person in charge to meet came
I came to see the person in charge of sales.

Ⓑ 이쪽으로 오십시오.
this way please come
Please come this way.

여기 고객 관리 책임자가 누구입니까?
here customer managing person in charge who be
Who is in charge of customer service here?

제가 판매 담당입니다.
I sales in charge be
I am in charge of sales.

Ⓐ 어떻게 오셨습니까? 무슨 일이십니까?
how came what business be
Whom are you here to see? May I help you?

Ⓑ 홍보부 김진수 부장님을 뵈러 왔는데요.
PR manager Kim Jinsu to meet came
I came to see Mr. Kim Jinsu in PR.

○ **약속하고 오셨습니까?**

appointment made and came

Do you have an appointment?

○ **성함이 어떻게 되세요?**

name how be

May I please have your name?

○ **인사부 김 부장님 뵈러 왔는데요.**

HR manager Kim to see came

I came to see Ms./Mr. Kim in HR.

○ **앉아서 기다리세요.**

please sit and wait

Please have a seat while you wait.

○ **여기서 기다리시면 됩니다.**

here can wait

You may wait here.

○ **기다리시게 해서 죄송합니다.**

let wait sorry

I'm sorry to have kept you waiting.

○ **다시 뵙게 되어 반갑습니다.**

again to see glad

It's nice to see you again.

Serving Refreshments 02

Ⓐ 차는 어떤 걸로 준비해 드릴까요?
tea for what prepare
What would you like to drink?

Ⓑ 아무거나 주세요.
anything please give
Anything is fine.

차 한 잔 하시겠어요?
tea one cup would have
Would you like something to drink?
Would you like some tea?

시원한 거 드릴까요?
cool thing shall give
Can I get you something cool to drink?

차가운 거 드릴까요, 따뜻한 거 드릴까요?
cold thing shall give, hot thing shall give
Would you like something cold or hot?

마실 것 좀 내오겠습니다.
thing to drink a little will bring
I'll bring something to drink.

저, 물 한 잔만 주시겠어요?
well water only one glass will give
Could I please just have a glass of water?

A 뭐뭐 있어요?
what what there be
What do you have?
What are my choices?

B 커피, 차, 주스가 있습니다.
coffee tea juice there be
We have coffee, tea, and juice.

음료수가 다 떨어졌습니다.
drinks all ran out
We are all out of drinks.

- **인스턴트 커피밖에 없는데 괜찮으시겠습니까?**
  instant coffee only there not be will be alright
  We only have instant coffee; will that be alright?

- **내린 커피 괜찮으시겠습니까?**
  brewed coffee will be alright
  Will brewed coffee be alright?

- **얼른 가서 사오겠습니다.**
  promptly go and buy come
  I'll go and buy some right now.

Dealing with Orders 03

Ⓐ 이 제품을 주문하려고 하는데 재고가 얼마나 있습니까?
this product intend to order stock how much there be
I would like to order this product; how much do you have in stock?

Ⓑ 죄송하지만 그 제품은 품절입니다.
sorry but the product out of stock be
I'm sorry, but this product is sold out.

AA사의 제품을 주문하고 싶습니다.
AA Company's product want to order
I want to order AA Company's product.

- 우선 1,000개를 주문하고 싶은데 재고가 있습니까?
  first 1,000 pieces want to order stock there be
  I'd like first to order 1,000 pieces; do you have that in stock?

- 얼마나 주문하실 겁니까?
  how much will order
  How much will you order?

- 그 물건은 재고가 많습니다.
  the product stock a lot
  We have plenty of this item in stock.

- 충분한 물량을 확보하고 있습니다.
  sufficient quantities secure
  We have secured sufficient quantities.

- 그 물건은 단종된 제품입니다.
  the product discontinued product be
  This item has been discontinued.

- 주문하신 모델은 더 이상 생산되지 않는 제품입니다.
  ordered model more not produced product be
  The model you ordered is no longer being produced.

- 언제쯤 새로 입고됩니까?
  about when newly stocked
  When will they be back in stock?

- 샘플을 본 후에 주문하겠습니다.
  sample after looking will order
  I will order after looking at a sample.

- 샘플을 몇 가지 보내 드리겠습니다.
  sample a few kind will send
  I will send you a few samples.

A 통관절차가 까다롭습니까?
customs clearance strict
Is it difficult to get them through customs?

B 아기 용품은 통관절차가 좀 까다로운 편입니다.
baby products customs clearance a little sort of strict
Getting products for babies through customs is a bit tricky.

통관하는 데 시간이 얼마나 걸립니까?
to pass through customs time how much take
How long will it take to get through customs?

주문할 때 20%를 선금으로 내셔야 합니다.
when order 20% pre-payment should pay
You have to put 20% down when ordering.

운송 비용과 절차는 어떻게 됩니까?
transportation expense and procedure how
What about shipping costs and procedures?

Caution

Don't write people's names in red

Koreans think it is bad to write people's names in red. In the past, writing a person's name in red on an official document meant he was either being deleted or that he had committed a crime. This is most likely the reason even today people disapprove of writing names in red.

Order Changes, Exchanges, and Refunds 04

A 지금 주문 변경을 해도 될까요?
now order can change
Can I change my order now?

B 어떻게 변경하시겠습니까?
how will change
How would you like to change it?

주문 수량을 변경하고 싶은데요.
order quantity want to change
I would like to change the quantity ordered.

주문 모델을 변경하고 싶은데요.
order model want to change
I would like to change the model I ordered.

A 보내 주신 물건이 주문한 것과 다릅니다.
sent product with ordered thing different
The item you sent me is not what I ordered.

B 죄송합니다. 착오가 있었습니다. 다시 보내 드리겠습니다.
sorry mistake there be again will send
I am sorry. There must have been some mistake. I will resend them.

물건을 받아보니 샘플보다 질이 떨어지네요.
product receive than sample quality debased
I received the items, but they are of a lower quality than the samples.

운반 과정에서 물건이 손상된 것 같습니다.
from transportation process product seem damaged
I think they were damaged during delivery.

보상액을 얼마나 지불하실 건지 궁금합니다.
compensation amount how much will pay wonder
I am wondering how much you will pay in compensation.

손해배상을 원합니다.
damage compensation want
We would like to be compensated for the damage.

손상된 제품은 당사가 전부 책임을 지도록 하겠습니다.
damaged product our company all responsibility will take
Our company will take complete responsibility for all damaged goods.

○ **물건에 하자가 있으면 바로 교환해 드리겠습니다.**

product flaw if there be immediately will exchange

If there are any problems with the items, we will exchange them immediately.

○ **착불로 보내시면 교환해 드리겠습니다.**

by payment on delivery if send will exchange

If you return them COD, we will exchange them for you.

○ **귀사의 클레임은 인정할 수 없습니다.**

your company's claim cannot admit

We are unable to accept your company's claim.

○ **손님, 정말 죄송합니다.**

customer really sorry

Ma'am/Sir, I am very sorry.

○ **착오가 있었던 것 같습니다. 불편을 드려 죄송합니다.**

mistake seem there be inconvenience give sorry

There seems to have been a mistake. I apologize for the inconvenience.

○ **당장 조사하여 답변을 드리도록 하겠습니다.**

quickly investigate answer will give

I will look into it and get back to you right away.

○ **기다리시게 해서 죄송합니다.**

let wait sorry

I'm sorry to have kept you waiting.

Delivery Delays · Payment Problems 05

A 주문한 물건이 아직 도착 안 했습니다.
ordered product yet not arrived
The products I ordered still haven't been delivered.

B 죄송합니다. 확인해 보고 다시 전화 드리겠습니다.
sorry check and again will call
I am sorry. I will look into it and call you back.

주문한 물건이 아직 안 왔습니다.
ordered product yet not came
The items I ordered still haven't arrived.

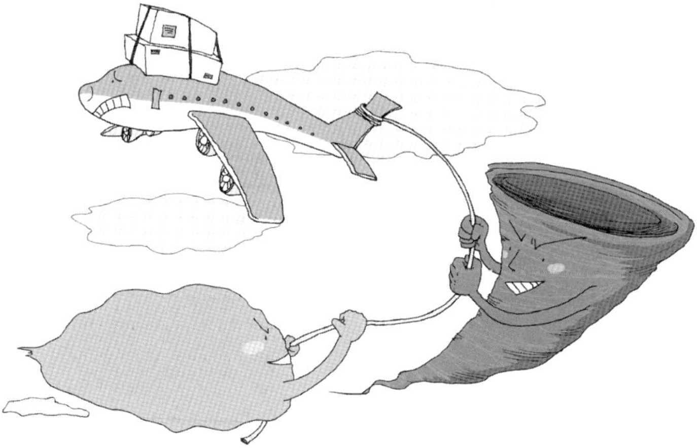

확인해 보고 바로 보내 드리겠습니다.
check and immediately will send
I will confirm this and send them to you immediately.

다음 주에 발송됩니다.
next week dispatched
They will be sent next week.

태풍 때문에 선적이 지연되고 있습니다.
because of typhoon shipping being delayed
The shipment is being delayed due to a typhoon.

5월 15일에 선적되었습니다.
on May 15th shipped
They were shipped on May 15th.

6월 5일에 베이징에 도착할 예정입니다.
on June 5th in Beijing to arrive schedule be
They are set to arrive in Beijing on June 5th.

A 송장에 액수가 잘못 기재됐습니다.
on invoice amount wrong stated
The amount on the invoice is incorrect.

B 정말 죄송합니다. 송장을 다시 만들어서 보내겠습니다.
really sorry invoice again will make and send
I am very sorry. I will correct the invoice and send it to you.

송장에 물량이 잘못 기재됐습니다.
on invoice quantity wrong stated
The quantity on the invoice is incorrect.

지불 기한이 2주 지났습니다.
payment deadline two weeks passed
The payment is two weeks overdue.

죄송합니다. 곧 결제해 드리겠습니다.
sorry soon will settle
I am sorry. I will make payment immediately.

이번 달 말까지 결제하겠습니다.
by this month end will settle
I will make payment by the end of this month.

The Aesthetics of Refusal

In Korea there are two types of refusals, which can make it difficult to decide on a proper response. For example, someone goes to a friend's house, only to find that they are in the middle of eating. In this situation, if the friend asks him or her to eat with them, nearly all Koreans will respond with something like "아닙니다. 먹고 왔습니다." or "점심을 늦게 먹어서 아직 배가 안 고픕니다." Despite these refusals, however, the owner of the house will usually continue to insist, and most often the guest will end up eating with the family.

Does this really mean that the guest winds up eating twice? This could be the case, but usually the guest has said he or she has eaten even when he or she has not. Thus such refusals can have two meanings. They can represent a true rejection of a counterpart's suggestion or offer, but they can also merely be made for the sake of etiquette. Even when someone is actually hungry and would like to eat, he or she will consider it polite to refuse two or three times before accepting. Conversely, when offering food to a Korean, even if he or she refuses at first, it is best to offer two or more times, just to be sure.

Warranties and After Service 06

제품 보증기간은 얼마나 됩니까?
product warranty period how long
How long is the warranty period for this product?

1년간 보증해 드립니다.
for one year give warranty
We provide a one-year warranty.

보증기간 동안 수리는 무료입니다.
during warranty period repair free of charge
Repairs are free during the warranty period.

보증기간이 지난 제품에 대해서는 부품비가 부과됩니다.
warranty period expired product regarding parts amount charged
You will have to pay for parts on products that are no longer under warranty.

Vocabulary

Industries

식품
food

광고
advertising

유통
distribution

IT
information technology

전자
electronics

가전
household appliances

기계
machine

중공업
heavy industries

조선
ship building

교육
education

건강
health

바이오
bio-chemical

의료기기
medical instruments

엔터테인먼트
entertainment

가구
furniture

물류
distribution

어업
fishing

광업
mining

건설
construction

제조
manufacturing

숙박업
lodging

의류
fashion

1 Directing Business Trips

2 Requesting and Approving Business Trips

3 Business Trip Reports

4 Transportation

5 Hotels

CHAPTER 10

Business Trips

Directing Business Trips 01

A 김 대리님, 이번 필리핀 무역 박람회에 좀 다녀와야겠는데요.
supervisor Kim to this Philippine Trade Fair should go and come
Ms./Mr. Kim, I think you should go to the upcoming Philippine Trade Fair.

B 네, 알겠습니다. 며칠부터 며칠까지입니까?
yes understood from what date to what date be
Alright. What are the dates?

- **출장 좀 다녀와요.**
  business trip please go and come
  You should go on a business trip.

- **이번 달 13일부터 15일까지 출장 좀 다녀올 수 있죠?**
  this month from 13th to 15th business trip can go and come
  You are available to go on a business trip from the 13th to the 15th of this month, right?

- **북미 지역은 김 과장이 담당이니까 이번 건은 김 과장이 갔다 오도록 하세요.**
  North America area manager Kim in charge this case manager Kim go and come
  Since you are in charge of North America, Ms./Mr. Kim, you should go this time.

이번 광고는 뉴질랜드에서 촬영합니다. 부장님께서 다녀오시면 좋겠는데요.
this ad in New Zealand shoot manager if go and come would be good
We are filming this ad in New Zealand. I would really like you to go.

A 이번 두바이 출장은 누가 가면 좋겠습니까?
this Dubai business trip who go would be good
Who should go on this business trip to Dubai?

B 프로젝트 담당자인 김 과장님이 가는 게 좋겠습니다.
project person in charge manager Kim go would be good
Ms./Mr. Kim is in charge of the project, so she/he should go.

누구를 보내면 좋을까요?
who if send would be good
Whom should we send?

중국어에 능한 김수진 씨가 가는 게 좋습니다.
Chinese proficient Kim Sujin go be good
Ms. Kim Sujin is good at Chinese so she should go.

꼼꼼하고 정확한 이 대리님이 적임자인 것 같습니다.
meticulous and precise supervisor Lee well qualified person seem
Ms./Mr. Lee is meticulous and precise; I think she/he is most qualified.

김민호 씨가 가면 되겠네요.
Mr. Kim Minho if go would be good
Well then, Mr. Kim Minho can go.

제가 다녀오겠습니다.
I will go and come
I'll go.

A 출장가기 전에 저쪽 담당자하고 미리 인사라도 해 놓는 게 좋겠습니다.
before going on a business trip with that side counterpart in advance greeting do would be good
Before you go on a business trip, you should say hi to the person in charge of that area.

B 네, 그렇게 하겠습니다.
yes so will do
Yes, I'll do that.

주말 끼워서 갔다 오도록 하세요.
weekend insert go and come
Please make the trip over the weekend.

이번에 간 김에 신상품 소싱과 미국 마트, 홈쇼핑, 백화점 시장 조사도 좀 해 오세요.

this time once go new product sourcing and the US mart home shopping department market research please do

While you're there, please also look into sourcing and do some market research on the US wholesale marts, home shopping, and department stores.

가서 꼭 입찰 성사되도록 하고 오세요.

go and surely bidding make achieved and come

Go and be sure to make a successful bid.

일처리 잘 하고 오세요.

handling well do and come

Go and do a good job.
Go and take care of business.

지시하신 대로 하겠습니다.

as directed will do

I'll do as you directed.

네, 완벽한 작품을 만들고 오겠습니다.

yes perfect piece make and come

I'll create a masterpiece.
I'll take care of everything.

Requesting and Approving Business Trips 02

Before going on business trips, you must first fill out a detailed plan and have it approved. The forms for the plans differ according to company, and should include specific directions and be submitted to a direct supervisor.

Ⓐ **5월 3일부터 7일까지 미국 샬롯 식품박람회에 좀 다녀왔으면 합니다.**
from May 3rd to 7th to the US Charlotte food fair a little want to go and come
I would like to go to the US for the food fair in Charlotte from May 3rd to 7th.

Ⓑ **출장계획서를 작성해서 올리세요.**
business trip proposal draw and present
Please fill out and turn in a business trip plan form.

출장 가서 뭘 할 건지 일별로 계획 세워 오세요.

business trip go what will do daily basis plan set up and come

Please make a plan for what you will do on each day of the business trip.

아직 출장 승인이 안 났습니다.

yet business trip approval not accepted

We still haven't received approval for a business trip.

Korean Accommodations

Hotels

Korean hotels are essentially the same as those elsewhere in the world.

Condominiums

Called "condo" for short, these are built like apartments, purchased privately, and then rented out by management companies for profit when the owners are not using them.

Youth Hostels

These are not as nice as hotels, but they are affordable and give guests a chance to mingle. This makes them popular with younger travelers.

Private Homes

These are private homes in which the owners rent out a room or two to travelers.

Pensions

These are smaller buildings. They are as nice as hotels but with a more house-like atmosphere that can accommodate an entire family.

Guest Houses

These are often in traditional Korean houses and offer guests a chance to experience Korean culture. These most often offers shared use of bathrooms, kitchen, and laundry rooms.

Home Stay

Staying with a Korean family offers opportunities to experience contemporary everyday living.

Business Trip Reports 03

When making a report following a business trip, be sure to understand exactly what your superiors expect. Some will want to see a detailed report of everything that happened, while others will want only the most important details and results.

A 갔다 온 일은 어떻게 됐습니까?
went and came work how became
How did the trip go?

B 네, 그럭저럭 잘 된 것 같습니다.
yes somehow well done seem
Well, I think it went rather well.

잘 다녀왔습니까?
well went and came
Did you have a good trip?

일은 잘됐습니까?
work well done
Did things go well?

일단 구두로 보고하도록 하세요.
for now verbal report do
First of all, please give us an oral report.

결과는 목요일 회의 때 보고 드리도록 하겠습니다.

result at Thursday meeting will report

I will give you full report of the results at Thursday's meeting.

촬영한 것은 편집, 녹음을 빨리해서 일주일 후 시사하도록 준비하겠습니다.

shoot thing edit record make haste one week later to preview will prepare

I will quickly edit and record sound for what we filmed, then have it ready for a preview within a week.

이번 촬영은 날씨 때문에 하루 늦어졌습니다만 결과는 잘 나왔습니다.

this shoot because of weather one day delayed but result well came out

Filming was delayed a day due to weather, but the results were good.

오늘까지 출장보고서 작성해야 돼요.

by today business trip report should write

I have to finish my business trip report by today.

A **출장비 정산은 어떻게 합니까?**

business trip expense settle how do

How do I settle the expenses from the business trip?

B **사내 출장시스템에 입력하고 전자결재하면 됩니다.**

in internal business trip system enter and electronic approval do

You can enter them in the company's business trip system and receive electronic approval.

유흥비는 인정이 안 됩니다.

entertainment expense approval not possible

Entertainment expenses are not covered.

비용 처리하는 방법 좀 가르쳐 주세요.

expense process method please teach

Please teach me how to process these expenses.

Transportation 04

KTX are the fastest trains in Korea, but there are also the Saemaeul and Mugunghwa trains. By KTX you can get from Seoul to Daegu in about one hour and forty minutes. To buy tickets in advance you can call 1544-7788 or 1588-7788 (Korail), or go to the Website www.korail.com.

A **KTX 서울에서 동대구 두 장 주세요.**
KTX from Seoul to Dongdaegu two tickets please give
Please give me two KTX tickets for Seoul to East Daegu.

B **몇 시 기차로 하시겠습니까?**
what time for train will have
What time would you like to depart?

제일 빨리 출발하는 걸로 주세요.
most early depart thing please give
Please give me the earliest departure.

특실로 두 장 주세요.
for executive car two tickets please give
Please give me two tickets for the executive car.
Please give me two first class tickets.

순방향석으로 주세요.
forward seat please give
Please give me a forward-facing seat.

역방향석으로 주세요.
backward seat please give
Please give me a backward-facing seat.

동반석으로 주세요.
companion seat please give
Please give us adjoining seats.

Ⓐ 서울에서 부산까지 KTX 요금이 얼마입니까?
from Seoul to Busan KTX fare how much be
How much is a KTX ticket from Seoul to Busan?

Ⓑ 51,200원입니다.
51,200 won be
It is 51,200 won.

서울에서 광주까지 시간이 얼마나 걸립니까?
from Seoul to Gwangju time how much take
How long does it take from Seoul to Gwangju?

몇 시에 도착해요?
at what time arrive
What time does it arrive?

서울에서 대구까지 한 시간 사십분쯤 걸립니다.
from Seoul to Daegu about one hour forty minutes take
It takes one hour and forty minutes from Seoul to Daegu.

역방향석을 구매하시면 할인을 받을 수 있습니다.
backward seat if purchase discount can get
If you take a backward-facing seat, you can get a discount.

Ⓐ **타는 곳이 어디예요?**

get on place where be

Where do I get on?

Ⓑ **14번 플랫폼으로 가세요.**

to number 14 platform please go

Please go to platform 14.

이 열차 부산 가는 기차 맞습니까?

this train Busan go train right

Is this the train to Busan?

네, 맞습니다.

yes right

Yes, that's right.

기차를 놓쳤어요.

train missed

I missed the train.

○ **더 빨리 출발하는 비행기는 없습니까?**

earlier depart airplane there not be

Isn't there a plane that leaves earlier?

○ **좀 더 늦게 출발하는 비행기는 없습니까?**

a little late depart airplane there not be

Isn't there a plane that leaves a bit later?

Ⓐ **한국에는 얼마나 체류할 예정입니까?**

in Korea how long stay plan be

How long do you plan to stay in Korea?

Ⓑ **일주일 동안 있을 겁니다.**

for one week will be

I will be here for one week.

○ **여권 좀 보여 주시겠습니까?**

passport would show

Will you please show me your passport?

○ **방문 목적이 무엇입니까?**

visit purpose what be

What is the purpose of your visit?

○ **업무차 왔습니다.**

on business came

I'm here on business.

○ **일 때문에 왔습니다.**

because of work came

I came for work.

Hotels 05

A 12월 23일부터 3박 예약하고 싶은데요.
from December 23rd three nights want to make reservation
I would like to make a reservation for three nights starting December 23rd.

B 죄송하지만 23일부터 25일은 예약이 꽉 차서 어렵습니다.
sorry but from 23rd to 25th reservation full difficult
I'm sorry, but that will be difficult as we are fully booked from the 23rd to the 25th.

웨이팅 걸어 드릴까요?
waiting shall list
Shall I put you on the waiting list?

지금은 성수기라서 방을 구하기가 어려워요.
now because peak season room finding difficult
It's peak season now, so it will be hard to find a room.

침대방으로 하시겠습니까, 온돌방으로 하시겠습니까?
with bed room will do with ondol room will do
Would you like a room with a bed, or a Korean traditional *ondol*?

Ⓐ **1박 요금이 어떻게 됩니까?**
one night fare how much
How much is it per night?

Ⓑ **스위트룸으로 하시면 1박에 17만 원입니다.**
for suite room if do at one night 170,000 won be
It is 170,000 won per night for a suite room.

조식이 포함된 요금입니까?
breakfast included fare be
Does that price include breakfast?

조식이 포함되지 않은 요금입니다.
breakfast not included fare be
That price does not include breakfast.

Ⓐ 예약하셨습니까?

reservation made

Did you make a reservation?

Ⓑ 네, 마이클 스미스로 예약했습니다.

yes for Michael Smith made reservation

Yes, I made a reservation under Michael Smith.

체크인하려고 하는데요.

want to check in

I would like to check in.

룸서비스를 이용하고 싶습니다.

room service want to use

I would like to order room service.

내일 아침 6시에 모닝콜 해 주세요.

tomorrow morning at six o'clock wake-up call please do

Please give me a wake-up call tomorrow at 6a.m.

Top Tourist Destinations in Seoul

Insa-dong: This is a "cultural street" that stretches from Jongno 2-ga street to Anguk-dong. There are plenty of cultural, artistic, and culinary delights to be enjoyed here (http://www.insadong.info).

Samcheong-dong: Here you can see both traditional Korean houses and homes from the 1960s and 70s. There are also many exotic restaurants and stores.

Cheonggyecheon: The Cheonggyecheon Stream, long paved over, was uncovered and reconstructed in 2005. It is a 3.6km long stream flowing along the boundary between the Jongno-gu and Jung-gu districts of downtown Seoul. It is a beautiful oasis in the middle of the city for walks and other activities (http://www.cheonggyecheon.or.kr).

Hongdae: "Hongdae" is short for Hongik Daehakgyo, or Hongik University. In front of this university are many cute stores and upscale coffee houses. At night it is a prime spot for clubs and other forms of entertainment.

Itaewon: This is the "representative" area for foreigners in Seoul. There are stores selling both imported products and Korean products for export. It also boasts the highest number of international restaurants and bars.

Myeong-dong: Myeong-dong is right outside the number 6 exit of the Euljiro-ipgu subway station, and boasts a huge variety of things to see, buy, eat, and drink.

Apgujeong: Apgujeong is popular among tourists for its many exotic cafés and stores selling expensive imported goods. If you are lucky, you may also see many famous Korean entertainers walking its streets and back alleys.

Vocabulary

Travel

자유 여행
free tour/not-guided tour

패키지여행
package tour/guided tour

에어텔
package with plane ticket and hotel

배낭여행
backpacking

성수기
peak season

비수기
off-season

왕복
round-trip

편도
one-way

항공권
plane ticket

조식
breakfast

중식
lunch

석식
dinner

숙박 시설
accommodations

민박
homestay

펜션
pension

관광
tour

관광객
tourist

관광지
tourist attraction

입장료
admission (fee)

일정
itinerary/schedule

여행 경비
travel expenses

비용
cost/expense

당일치기 여행
one-day trip

여행사
travel agency

가이드/인솔자
tour guide

여행자 보험
traveler's insurance

현지식
local meal

선택 관광
option tour

유류할증료
fuel surcharge

공항세
airport tax

여권
passport

수하물/짐
luggage

기내용 가방
carry-on bag

출발
departure

도착
arrival

편명
flight

국내선
domestic flight

국제선
international flight

1 At the Airport

2 Tour Guides

3 Buying Meals

4 Drinking

5 Gifts

6 Expressing Thanks

CHAPTER 11

Entertaining Customers

At the Airport 01

A 혹시 권현성 이사님이십니까?
by any chance director Kwon Hyeonseong be
Are you Mr. Kwon Hyeonseong?

B 네, 그런데요.
yes so
Yes, I am.

혹시 김민호 씨 맞으십니까?
by any chance Mr. Kim Minho right
Are you Mr. Kim Minho?

저는 사성물산의 이명진입니다.
I Sasung Corporation Lee Myeongjin be
I am Lee Myeongjin from Sasung Corporation.

오래 기다리셨죠?
long time waited
You waited a long time, didn't you?

아니요, 저도 방금 왔습니다.
no I also now came
No, I arrived just now.

Ⓐ **이번에 LA에 계시는 동안 제가 모시게 되었습니다.**
this time in LA while being I became serve
I will be taking care of you during your stay in LA.

Ⓑ **잘 부탁합니다.**
well ask
Thank you.

한국에 오신 걸 환영합니다.
to Korea came welcome
Welcome to Korea.

장시간 비행으로 피곤하시겠습니다.
due to long time flight must be tired
You must be tired after such a long flight.

오시느라 피곤하시겠습니다.
to come must be tired
You must be tired from your trip.

먼 길 오시느라 고생하셨습니다.

far way come suffered

You had a long hard trip.

김민호 사장님을 모시게 되어 영광입니다.

president Kim Minho host become honored

It's an honor to host you President Kim.

A 가방은 제가 들겠습니다.

bag I will carry

Let me take your bags.

B 아, 괜찮습니다.

ah alright

Oh, that's alright.

제가 묵으실 호텔까지 모시겠습니다.

I to stay to hotel will take

I will take you to your hotel.

이쪽으로 가시죠.

this way let's go

Let's go this way.

주차장에 차를 주차해 두었습니다.

in parking lot car parked

I left the car in the parking lot.

죄송합니다만, 차가 고장 나서 택시로 가셔야 할 것 같습니다.
sorry but car broke down by taxi should go seem
I'm sorry, but the car is broken. It looks like we'll have to take a taxi.

택시로 모시게 돼서 죄송합니다.
by taxi to serve sorry
I'm sorry that we have to go by taxi.

A 뉴욕에 머무시는 동안 필요한 게 있으시면 뭐든지 저한테 말씀하시면 됩니다.
in New York while staying needed thing if there be anything to me can say
Just let me know if there is anything you need during your stay in New York.

B 잘 부탁 드립니다.
well ask
Thank you very much.

뉴욕 방문은 처음이신가요?
New York visit first time be
Is this your first visit to New York?

얼마 만에 뉴욕에 오셨습니까?
how long time to New York came
How long has it been since your last trip to New York?

A 체류하실 호텔이 어디죠?
to stay hotel where be
Where is the hotel you will be staying?

B 시청 앞에 있는 플라자호텔입니다.
in front of city hall Plaza Hotel be
It's Plaza Hotel, in front of City Hall.

- 한림호텔에 방을 예약해 두었습니다.
  at Hollym Hotel room booked
  I reserved a room at Hollym Hotel.

- 묵으시는 호텔에서 회사까지는 걸어서 10분 거리입니다.
  from staying hotel to company by walk ten minute distance be
  It's a ten-minute walk to the company from your hotel.

- 체크인 하시는 거 도와드릴까요?
  check in will help
  May I help you get checked in?

A 내일 몇 시에 모시러 올까요?
tomorrow what time at to pick up will come
What time shall I pick you up tomorrow?

B 괜찮습니다. 제가 회사로 찾아가겠습니다.
alright I to company will go
That's alright. I'll go to the office on my own.

푹 쉬십시오.
well please rest
Please get some rest.

편히 쉬십시오.
comfortably please rest
Please have a comfortable stay.

내일 9시에 호텔 로비로 모시러 오겠습니다.
tomorrow at nine to hotel lobby to pick up will come
I will come pick you up in the hotel lobby tomorrow at 9a.m.

아침 8시까지 로비에서 기다려 주세요.
morning by eight at lobby please wait
Please wait for me by 8a.m. in the hotel lobby.

A 서울에서 머무시는 동안 불편한 점은 없으셨는지 모르겠습니다.
in Seoul while staying uncomfortable thing there not be not know
I hope you weren't at all uncomfortable during your stay in Seoul.

B 아닙니다. 세심하게 신경 써 주셔서 감사했습니다.
no carefully paid attention thanked
Not at all. Thank you for taking such good care of me.

다음에 오실 때는 더 좋은 곳으로 모시겠습니다.
next time come to better place will take
We'll find you a nicer place to stay on your next visit.

덕분에 잘 지내다 갑니다.
thanks to (you) well stayed and go
I had a pleasant stay, thanks to you.

Ⓐ 서울에 계시는 동안 가 보시고 싶은 곳이 있으십니까?
in Seoul while being want to go place there be
Are there any places you want to go while you are in Seoul?

Ⓑ 글쎄요. 인사동에 한번 가 보고 싶네요.
well to Insa-dong once want to go
Well, I would like to go to Insa-dong once.

가 보시고 싶은 곳이 있으시면 제가 모시겠습니다.
want to go place if there be I would take
If there is anywhere you would like to go, I will take you.

일정이 빡빡해서 몇 군데 못 갈 것 같습니다.

schedule tight few place cannot go seem

Our schedule is so tight that I don't think we'll be able to visit more than a few places.

오전에 마케팅부 신제품 설명회에 참석하시고, 오후에는 서울 시내를 관광하실 예정입니다.

in the morning Marketing department to new product briefing attend in the afternoon Seoul downtown see plan

Our plan is in the morning to go to the meeting to explain the new products at the Marketing department, and in the afternoon to sightsee in downtown Seoul.

시티투어를 하시면 편하게 서울 시내를 둘러보실 수 있습니다.

city tour if do comfortably Seoul downtown can look around

If you take a city tour, you can comfortably see all of downtown Seoul.

Going for Round Two

When people get together for dinner and drinks in Korea, they tend to move around to a few different places. When this happens, the places are referred to as "1차, 2차, 3차 (round 1, 2, and 3)." For example, if a group goes to a restaurant for dinner, a beer hall after that, and a singing room to finish up, they might say "We spent round one at a restaurant, round two at a beer hall, and round three at a singing room." And you will often hear the expression "2차 갑시다." This more or less means "Let's go somewhere else and enjoy a new atmosphere."

Buying Meals

03

When Koreans take customers out for meals, they often go to high-end Japanese restaurants or Korean restaurants that specialize in grilled meats. These establishments usually provide quiet private rooms, making them ideal for discussing business over food and drinks. Most of these rooms have traditional floor seating, as opposed to tables and chairs, and many people believe this more traditional, and familiar atmosphere aids in building closeness and trust among people. When assigning seats, the guests should be seated on the inside, furthest from the door.

A **뭘 좋아하십니까?**
what like
What do you like?

B **다 좋아합니다.**
all like
I like everything.

뭘 드시겠습니까?
what would eat
What would you like to eat?

혹시 못 드시는 것 있으십니까?
by any chance cannot eat thing there be
Is there anything you don't eat?

○ **혹시 매운 것도 드실 수 있으십니까?**

by any chance spicy thing also can eat

Can you eat spicy food?

○ **가리는 것 없습니다.**

choosy thing there not be

I eat everything.

○ **더 필요한 것 있으세요?**

more need thing there be

Do you need anything else?

○ **이건 좀 매운데 괜찮으시겠습니까?**

this a little spicy but would be fine

This is a bit spicy; will that be alright?

Drinking 04

Drinking is widespread in Korea, but so are police checkpoints. If you plan on drinking, leave the car at the office or use "대리운전," a driving service. Driving services are very convenient and inexpensive; with a single phone call, you can quickly have someone show up to drive you home in your own car.

A 술은 뭘로 하시겠습니까?
alcohol for what would do
What sort of alcohol would you like to drink?

B 소주 빼고 다 잘 마십니다.
except soju all well drink
I like everything except soju.

안주는 뭘로 드시겠습니까?
side dish for what would eat
What side dishes would you like with your drinks?

제가 한잔 따르겠습니다.
I one glass will pour
Let me pour you a drink.

A 건배!
cheers
Cheers!/Bottoms up!

B 위하여!
for
Cheers!

원샷!
bottoms up
One shot!/Bottoms up!

우리 회사의 발전을 위하여!
our company's development for
Here's to our company's development!

총무부를 위하여!
General Affairs department for
Here's to the General Affairs department!

전략개발팀을 위하여!
Strategy department for
Here's to the Strategy Development team!

자, 다들 잔 비웠습니까?
well all glass emptied
Well, have you all emptied your glasses?

김 대리 잔이 비었네요.
supervisor Kim glass empty
I see Ms./Mr. Kim's glass is empty.

모두 잔을 채우세요.
all glass please fill
Everyone fill your glass.

A 괜찮으세요?
alright
Are you alright?

B 머리가 아파서 이제 그만 마셔야겠습니다.
head ache now no more will drink
My head hurts so I will stop drinking now.

알딸딸하니 기분이 좋네요.
feel buzzed feeling good
I'm a bit buzzed and feeling good.

- **취하네요.**
  feel buzzed
  I'm getting drunk.

- **딱 좋네요.**
  perfectly good
  I'm just right.

- **어질어질합니다.**
  feel dizzy
  I feel a bit dizzy.

- **속이 안 좋아서 더 못 마시겠습니다.**
  feel sick no more can drink
  I feel queezy so I shouldn't drink any more.

- **토하고 나면 좀 나을 거예요.**
  after throw up a little will be better
  You'll feel better after you throw up.

- **내일 아침에 해장국을 드시면 속이 좀 풀리실 겁니다.**
  tomorrow morning hangover soup once eat stomach will be cool down
  If you have some hangover soup in the morning, your stomach will feel better.

- **제가 댁까지 모실 테니 걱정하지 마시고 맘껏 드십시오.**
  I to home will take don't worry as much as drink
  I'll take you home, so don't worry and drink as much as you like.

A 주량이 어떻게 되십니까?
drinking capacity how much
How much can you drink?

B 소주 한 병 정도 마십니다.
soju about one bottle drink
I can drink about a bottle of soju.

얼마나 드십니까?
how much drink
How much do you drink?

끝없이 마실 수 있어요.
endless can drink
I can keep on drinking forever.

그 사람은 주당이에요.
that man heavy drinker be
She/He is a heavy drinker.

숙취 때문에 다음날 고생했어요.
because of hangover next day suffered
I suffered the next day because of a hangover.

전에 술을 너무 많이 마셔서 필름이 끊긴 적이 있습니다.
before alcohol too much drank once passed out
I once blacked out from drinking too much alcohol.

건강 때문에 술을 끊었습니다.
health because of alcohol quit
I gave up drinking for my health.

Ⓐ **2차 안 가요?**
second round won't go?
Shall we go to round two?

Ⓑ **2차 좋지요.**
second round good
Round two sounds good.

어디 가서 한잔 더 합시다.
somewhere go one more drink let's have
Let's go somewhere and have another drink.

내일 아침 일찍 회의가 있어서 이제 그만 일어나야겠습니다.
tomorrow early morning meeting there be now should leave
I have a meeting early tomorrow morning, so I should be going now.

누가 대리운전 번호 있어요?
who driving service number have
Who has the number for a driving service?

Drinking Culture: One Shot, Sharing Glasses, and Boilermakers

Koreans generally like to drink fast. When someone toasts by yelling "원샷!," it means they would like you to empty your glass in one gulp. This makes the entire group drink quickly and also feel a sense of bonding. "폭탄주 (boilermakers)" are a combination of two or more kinds of alcohol, and are enjoyed both for their particular taste and their ability to improve the atmosphere. At first boilermaker referred only to a combination of beer and whiskey, but now there are many varieties such as beer and soju (*somaek*) and soju and Baekseju (*osipseju*).

Gifts 05

High-priced gifts can actually be burdensome for the receiver, so companies most often give something with the company logo on it or a Korean tourist souvenir.

A **별것 아닙니다만, 감사의 표시로 준비했습니다.**
special thing not be however for expression of gratitude prepared.
It's really nothing, but we have prepared a token of our gratitude.

B **아, 뭐 이런 걸 다…….**
ah what like this all
Oh, well, I don't know what to say.

작은 성의니 받아 주시면 감사하겠습니다.
as little sincerity once receive would appreciate
We hope you will accept this small token of our gratitude.

회사에서 준비한 작은 기념품입니다.
company prepared little souvenir be
This is just a little souvenir our company prepared.

저희 회사 홍보물입니다.
our company PR material be
These are some PR materials from our company.

작은 선물을 준비했는데 마음에 드실지 모르겠습니다.
little present prepared if taking your fancy not know.
We prepared a small gift; we hope you will like it.

언제 이런 걸 다 준비하셨습니까?
when this all prepared
When did you have time to get this?

그럼 감사히 받겠습니다.
then with appreciation will receive
Well, thank you very much.

Expressing Thanks 06

Ⓐ 그동안 불편한 점이 없으셨나 모르겠습니다.
meanwhile uncomfortable thing if there not be not know
I hope you were not at all uncomfortable during your stay.

Ⓑ 여러 가지 많이 도와 주셔서 감사했습니다.
many things a lot help appreciated
Thank you for doing so much for me.

덕분에 좋은 시간 보냈습니다.
thanks to (you) had a good time
I had a great time, thanks to you.

친절하게 챙겨 주셔서 감사했습니다.
nicely taking care of thanked
Thank you for taking such good care of me.

그동안 신세 많이 졌습니다.
meanwhile owe a lot
You did a lot for me on this trip.

잘 놀다 갑니다.
well enjoyed and go
I had a great time.

구경 잘 했습니다.

look around well

I got to see a lot.

맛있게 잘 먹었습니다.

deliciously well ate

I ate a lot of delicious food.

음식도 맛있고 분위기도 좋았습니다.

food also delicious atmosphere was good

The food was delicious and the atmosphere was pleasant.

Caution

Don't pour alcohol with only one hand.

Unless it is with a very good friend or someone much younger, you should pour and receive alcohol with two hands. Also, when in front of a superior, you should turn your head to the side when drinking.

Vocabulary

Korean Food

불고기
grilled beef

갈비
grilled (beef) ribs

삼겹살
pork belly/bacon

삼계탕
chicken and ginseng stew

비빔밥
rice with mixed vegetables

돌솥비빔밥
rice with mixed vegetables in a hot stone pot

국수
noodles

물냉면
cold noodles in broth

비빔냉면
cold noodles mixed with hot sauce

된장찌개
bean paste stew

순두부찌개
soft tofu stew

부대찌개
military base stew
(stew with hams and baked beans)

설렁탕
beef soup

육개장
spicy beef and egg soup

생선구이
grilled fish

감자탕
pork and potato stew

해물탕
mixed seafood stew

잡채
sweet potato noodles with mixed vegetables

보쌈
steamed pork and spicy vegetables

제육볶음
spicy stir-fried pork

떡볶이
spicy rice cake

튀김
battered, deep-fried foods

순대
sausage filled with rice or noodles

오징어볶음
stir-fried squid and vegetables

Tastes

맛있다
delicious/to taste good

맛없다
not delicious/to taste bad

달다
sweet

쓰다
bitter

짜다
salty

맵다
spicy

시다
sour

싱겁다
bland

담백하다
savory

고소하다
nutty

시원하다
refreshing

달콤하다
sweet

새콤달콤하다
sweet and sour

짭짤하다
a bit salty

매콤하다
a bit spicy

얼큰하다
spicy

바삭바삭하다
crispy

쫄깃쫄깃하다
chewy

연하다
soft/tender

질기다
chewy/tough

1 Congratulations

2 Encouragement·Condolences

3 Invitations

4 Gatherings

5 Congratulatory Messages

6 Messages of Condolences

CHAPTER 12

Personal Relations

Congratulations 01

When invited to a wedding, it is customary to give cash as a gift; for new business openings either cash or flowers are acceptable. When company sends a gift, it is most often a large wreath of flowers.

A 현수 씨, 오늘 생일이시라면서요? 축하해요.
Hyeonsu today they said birthday congratulations
Hyeonsu, I hear it's your birthday today. Happy birthday.

B 고맙습니다. 오늘 제가 우리 부서 점심 살게요.
thank you today I our team buy lunch
Thank you. I'll buy lunch for our department today.

생일 축하합니다.
birthday congratulations
Happy birthday!

생신을 축하드립니다.
birthday congratulations (to seniors)
Happy birthday!

합격을 축하드립니다.
pass congratulations
Congratulations on passing.

결혼 축하합니다.

marriage congratulations

Congratulations on your marriage.

Ⓐ 부장님, 승진을 축하드립니다.

manager promotion congratulations

Congratulations on your promotion.

Ⓑ 고맙습니다. 여러분 덕분입니다.

thank you thanks to you

Thank you. It's all thanks to you guys.

부장으로 승진하신 걸 축하드립니다.

into manager promoted congratulations

Congratulations on your promotion to manager.

A 대구지점 개업식에 뭘 보내면 좋을까요?
Daegu branch at opening ceremony what if send would be good
What should we send for the opening of the Daegu branch?

B 축하 화환을 하나 보내도록 하세요.
celebration standing flower wreath one send
Please make sure to send a congratulatory wreath.

축하 카드를 보내야겠어요.
congratulations card should send
I should send a congratulatory card.

개업 축하 화분을 주문하려면 어디로 전화해야 하지요?
open business celebration flower pot to order to where call
Where should I call to get a potted plant to congratulate them on their new business?

이전 축하
relocation celebration
Congratulations on Your Relocation

창업 축하
foundation celebration
Congratulations on Your Opening

창립 10주년 축하
10th foundation year celebration
Congratulations on Your 10th Anniversary

Encouragement · Condolences 02

A 좀 어떠십니까?
a little how
How are you doing?

B 이제 많이 나아졌어요.
now a lot got better
I'm a lot better now.

힘내십시오.
cheer up/go for it
Cheer up.

불행 중 다행입니다.
midst of misfortune fortune be
You're very lucky (it isn't worse).

얼마나 고생이 되십니까?
how much hard
This must be very hard.

빨리 나으세요.
fast please get better
Get well soon.

조리 잘 하세요.
care well do
Take good care of yourself.

고생이 많으십니다.

hardship much be

You've been through a lot.

A 힘들어서 못 다니겠어요. 때려치울까 봐요.

as hard cannot go may quit

It's too hard to keep working. I'm thinking of quitting.

B 조금만 참읍시다.

just a little let's stand

Just be patient.

Hold out just a little bit longer.

이번 고비만 넘기면 또 괜찮아질 거예요.

only this hump if overcome again will be alright

You just need to get over this hump and everything will be alright.

힘냅시다.

let's cheer up

Let's cheer up.

Let's think positive.

더 어려운 일도 이겨냈잖아요.

more hard work overcame

You've been through worse.

그래, 그만 둬.

yes quit

Yes, just quit.

이거 아니면 할 거 없겠어?

this if not be thing to do there not be

You can do other things.

Housewarming Presents

"집들이" is the Korean word for a housewarming party. The owner of the new house prepares the food and drink, while the guests all bring gifts. Some do choose to bring decorations or daily necessities, but the following gifts are by far the most common: powdered or liquid detergents, with the hope that the owner's wealth and happiness will swell like foamy bubbles; rolls of toilet paper, with the wish that the owner's affairs will roll out smoothly; and candles, with the hope that the owner will rise like fire.

Invitations 03

For weddings, printed invitations are the norm, while for first year birthday parties, email is more common. Invitations to housewarming parties are usually done in person verbally.

신차 시승회가 있는데 오시면 감사하겠습니다.
new car test drive there be if come would appreciate
We are having a new car test driving event, and would be very grateful if you could come.

참석하셔서 자리를 빛내 주세요.
attend and place please honor
We would be very grateful if you could attend.

이번 신제품 론칭 행사에 초대합니다.
this new product launching event invite
You are invited to the launching of our new product.

저녁 만찬에 참가해 주시면 감사하겠습니다.
at dinner party if participate would appreciate
We would be grateful if you would attend our dinner party.

리셉션에 오셨으면 좋겠습니다.
to reception if come would be good
I would like it if you could come to the reception.

신년회에 참석해 주세요.
to New Year party please participate
Please come to our New Year's party.

송년회에 참석하시기를 바라겠습니다.

to end of the year party attend hope

I hope you will attend our end of the year party.

A 이번 주 토요일 저녁에 집에서 식사 대접을 하고 싶습니다.

this week Saturday evening at home dinner want to treat

I would like to have you over to my house for dinner this Saturday.

B 몇 시까지 가면 되나요?

by what time can come

What time should I be there?

금요일에 제 생일 파티가 있는데 오시겠어요?

on Friday my birthday party there be will (you) come

Friday night is my birthday party. Will you come?

별일 없으면 꼭 오세요.

special thing if there not be surely please come

If you are not busy, please do come.

다음 주 토요일에 우리 아이 돌잔치가 있는데, 오셔서 식사나 하고 가세요.

next week on Saturday our baby first birthday party there be please come and have meal

Next Saturday is our child's first birthday. Please come and dine with us.

저 결혼합니다. 다음 주 토요일입니다.

I marry next week Saturday be

I'm getting married. It's on next Saturday.

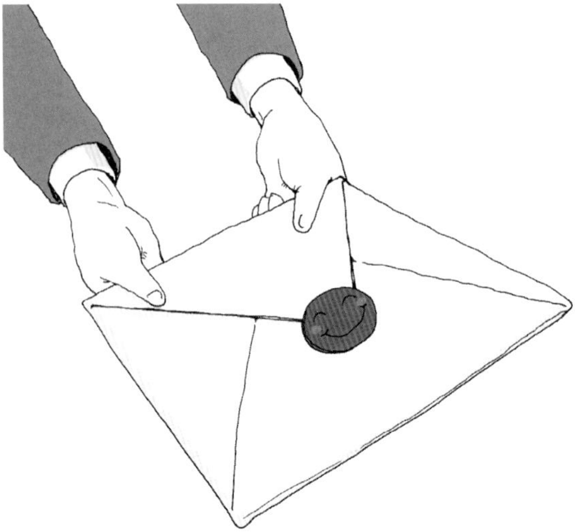

Ⓐ **오늘 한잔 할까요?**
today one drink shall do
Shall we have a drink today?

Ⓑ **미안해요. 오늘은 제가 선약이 있어서요.**
sorry today I previous engagement there be
Sorry. Today I have a previous engagement.

정말 죄송합니다. 그날 제가 중요한 약속이 있어서요.
really sorry that day I important appointment have
I am truly sorry. I have an important appointment that day.

다음에 한잔 합시다.
next time a drink let's have
Let's have a drink next time.

가고 싶은데 오늘은 시간 내기가 어렵겠습니다.

want to go but today time spare would be hard

I would like to go, but I don't have time today.

도저히 시간이 안 될 것 같아요.

no way time may not available

There is no way I will be able to make time.

Special Birthdays: 백일, 돌, 환갑, 칠순

The most important birthday celebrations in Korea occur after 100 days (백일), one year (돌), 60 years (환갑), and 70 years (칠순). The first two are to congratulate young infants on their health and growth, and to give good wishes for the future.

After one year, in particular, babies are dressed in "first-year clothing (돌복)," a special outfit for the occasion. Then things such as thread, a pen/pencil, a book, and money are placed in front of the baby, and whichever one the baby grabs is supposed to decide upon its future—this is called "first-year grabbing (돌잡이)." Thread means the baby will enjoy a long life; a pen/pencil or a book means the baby will become a scholar; and money means the baby will grow rich.

The 60th birthday is referred to as "환갑," while "칠순" is the name for the 70th. These are both special birthdays, since in the past 60 years was considered a very long life, and 70 was most uncommon. These days people live much longer, so the meaning has shifted somewhat. Rather than celebrating the end of a life, older married couples often use the occasion to go on a vacation together.

Gatherings 04

"회식" refers to any gathering where people from the same group or company eat and drink together. It is usually done with company funds, and intended to help members bond and become closer. Korean firms often have these gatherings when a new person joins the team, or a project has been successfully concluded. And even in the absence of these special events, regular gatherings are held to foster teamwork and camaraderie among employees. These gatherings can smooth out tensions that naturally arise in the office, and should not be missed.

Ⓐ 회식 날짜 잡혔어요?
gathering date set
Has the date for the gathering been set?

Ⓑ 날짜는 잡혔는데 회식 장소를 아직 못 정했어요.
date set but gathering place yet not decided
The date is set, but we don't have a place yet.

- 신입사원이 들어왔으니 환영회를 열어 줘야겠죠?
new employee came welcome party hold why not
We have a new employee so we should hold a welcoming gathering, right?

- 요즘 분위기도 안 좋은데 단합대회나 한번 합시다.
these days atmosphere not good one time gathering let's have
The atmosphere is not very good these days, so we should hold a gathering to boost solidarity.

- 회식이 너무 자주 있어서 살이 쪘어요.
gathering too frequent there be gained weight
We're having such frequent gatherings that I've gained some weight.

- 회식 자리에 자꾸 빠지는 건 좋지 않아요.
to gathering repeatedly skip not good
It's not good to skip gatherings too often.

A 2차는 노래방 어때요?

second round singing room how about

How about a singing room for round two?

B 노래방 좋지요.

singing room good

A singing room would be nice.

2차는 과장님이 쏘신대요.

second round manager will treat

The manager says she/he is paying for round two.

오늘 과장님이 한턱 내신대요.

today manager will treat

Today the manager said she/he is paying.

Arrangements for Happy and Sad Events

Koreans make special arrangements for occasions considered particularly happy or sad. Among these are weddings, funerals, and special birthdays. In Korea, it is not only family but also friends, coworkers, business associates, school alumni, and others who participate in these events.

There are many who even say that the success or failure of interpersonal relationships depends largely on how well a person takes care of his or her obligations on these special days. Worth mentioning here is that one of the primary obligations is a donation of money. It is customary to put cash into an envelope and deliver it as a token of congratulations or condolences as the occasion demands. The amount varies according to both the giver's closeness to the receiver and to his social and financial position.

Congratulatory Messages 05

Birthdays

- 쉰한 번째 생일을 진심으로 축하합니다.
  Heartfelt congratulations on your 51st birthday.

- 생신을 진심으로 축하하오며 건강과 행복을 기원합니다.
  Best wishes on your birthday and for your continued health and happiness.

- 아기의 백일을 축하하며 더욱 건강하게 자라길 기원합니다.
  Best wishes on your baby's 100th day and for continued healthy growth.

- 아기의 첫돌을 축하하며 귀엽고 튼튼하게 키우길 바랍니다.
  Congratulations on your baby's first birthday and may you continue to raise her/him cute and strong.

- 첫돌을 맞이한 아기에게 더없이 큰 사랑과 축복이 깃들기를 바랍니다.
  With love and blessings for your baby on her/his first birthday.

Weddings

- 결혼을 축하하며 두 분의 앞날에 사랑과 행복이 가득하시기를 기원합니다.
  Congratulations on your wedding, and may both of your futures be filled with love and happiness.

- 결혼을 축하하며 모든 이의 축복 속에 행복하게 살기 바랍니다.
  Best wishes on your marriage, and blessed by all may you live happily together.

- 기쁜 자리 함께 못하여 죄송합니다. 두 분 앞날에 밝은 웃음만 가득하기를 빕니다.
  Apologies for being unable to share this precious day. May the two of you enjoy a joyous future together.

Promotions

- 영전을 축하하며 높으신 뜻 새로이 펼치시기 바랍니다.
  Congratulations on your promotion, and may you once again achieve your lofty ideals.

- 영예로운 진급을 축하하며 무궁한 발전을 기원합니다.
  Congratulations on your honorable promotion, and may you see continued success.

- 진급을 축하하오며 더 큰 영광 있기를 기원합니다.
  Congratulations on your promotion, and may you achieve even greater honors.

Retirements

- 정년퇴임을 축하드리며 앞으로 더욱 건강하시기를 기원합니다.
  Best wishes for your retirement, and may you enjoy continued good health.

- 정년퇴임을 맞아 더욱 건강하시고 새로운 일 순조롭기를 기원합니다.
  On this occasion of your retirement, may you enjoy still better health and new successes.

Teachers' Day

- 저희들을 바른길로 이끌어주신 선생님, 감사합니다.
  Thank you for leading us along the proper path.

- 사랑으로 이끌어 주신 선생님의 가르침에 깊이 감사합니다.
  With deep gratitude for your loving guidance.

- 선생님, 멀리서 인사드림을 용서하시고 늘 즐겁고 건강하시길 바랍니다.
  Please forgive me for not delivering this in person and I wish you happiness and health.

- 언제나 저희들을 사랑하시던 선생님, 그 넓으신 마음 본받는 제자가 되겠습니다.
  With your constant love, we will endeavor to become worthy students.

Opening a New Business

- 오늘의 뜻깊은 개업이 무궁한 발전과 번영의 초석이 되기를 기원합니다.
  We hope today's opening will serve as the cornerstone for unlimited development and success.

- 하나님의 축복이 사업장 위에 넘치게 되기를 기원합니다.
  We pray that God's blessings will reign abundantly over your place of business.

- 개업을 축하하며 행운과 발전을 기원합니다.
  Congratulations on your new business, and best wishes for happiness and success.

- 개원을 축하하며 무궁한 번창을 기원합니다.
  Best wishes on the opening of your clinic, and for endless development.

개업을 축하하며 뜻한 일 모두 번창하시기 바랍니다.
Best wishes on the opening of your business, and for success in all your endeavors.

Births

득남을 축하하오며 산모의 건강을 기원합니다.
Congratulations on the birth of your son, and best wishes for the mother's health.

사랑스런 아기의 탄생을 축하하며 산모와 아기의 건강을 빕니다.
Congratulations on the birth of your lovely baby, and best wishes for the health of both baby and mother.

귀여운 공주님의 탄생을 축하하며 산모의 건강을 기원합니다.
Best wishes on the birth of your adorable princess, and for the health of her mother.

Moving

새 보금자리로 입주하심을 축하하며 가정의 건강과 행복을 기원합니다.
Congratulations on moving into your new home, and best wishes for the health and happiness of your family.

새 사옥으로의 이전을 축하하며 더 큰 발전 있기를 기원합니다.
Best wishes on moving into your new home, and for even greater successes.

새집 마련을 축하하며 새로운 마음으로 힘차게 나아가기를 기원합니다.
Congratulations on your new home, and for renewed energy and success.

보금자리 마련을 축하하며 화목한 가정 이루시기 바랍니다.
Congratulations on your new place, and best wishes for your family's peace and harmony.

Messages of Condolences 06

Illnesses

- 하루빨리 일어나셔서 이전보다 더욱 건강해지시기를 기원합니다.
  With best wishes for a speedy recovery and even better health than before.

- 편찮으시다는 소식 듣고 놀랐습니다. 하루빨리 건강을 되찾으시기 바랍니다.
  I was shocked at the news of your illness. Best wishes for a speedy recovery.

- 병환 속히 나으시어 건강한 모습으로 우리에게 돌아오시기를 기원합니다.
  Hoping you will return to us in good health following a speedy recovery.

Deaths

- 뜻밖의 비보에 슬픈 마음 금할 길 없습니다. 머리 숙여 고인의 명복을 빕니다.
  I cannot contain my grief at this unexpected and tragic news. Our solemn prayers are with you.

- 평소 고인의 은덕을 되새기며 삼가 고인의 명복을 빕니다.
  We remember the deceased's great virtue, and pray she/he may rest in peace.

- 큰 슬픔을 위로 드리오며 삼가 고인의 명복을 빕니다.
  Condolences on your great loss, and may the deceased rest in peace.

- 부득이한 사정으로 조문치 못하여 죄송하오며 삼가 고인의 명복을 빕니다.
  Apologies for being unable to attend the funeral, and prayers for the deceased's peaceful repose.

- 삼가 조의를 표하오며 주님의 위로와 소망이 함께 하기를 기원합니다.
  Our deepest condolences and prayers for Jesus' comfort and hope.

Caution

Don't point at people.

When referring to people it is impolite to point at them with one finger. Rather, the entire hand, palm facing upward, should be used. It is also a breach of etiquette to use the hands to indicate a superior should join you. You should walk over to a superior and escort him or her to the desired location.

Vocabulary

Drinks

양주
Western liquor

맥주
beer

생맥주
draft beer

와인/포도주
wine

소주
soju

막걸리
coarse rice ale

동동주
refined rice ale

정종
sake

청주
clear rice wine

매실주
plum wine

인삼주
ginseng wine

복분자주
wild rasberry wine

Side Dishes

해물파전
seafood and scallion pancake

두부김치
tofu and kimchi

골뱅이무침
seasoned ark shells

해물떡볶이
stir fried seafood and rice cakes

김치전
kimchi pancake

마른안주
dried snacks

과일안주
assorted fruit

홍합탕
mussels soup

해물탕
mixed seafood soup

조개탕
clam soup

오뎅탕
fish cake soup

알탕
fish roe soup

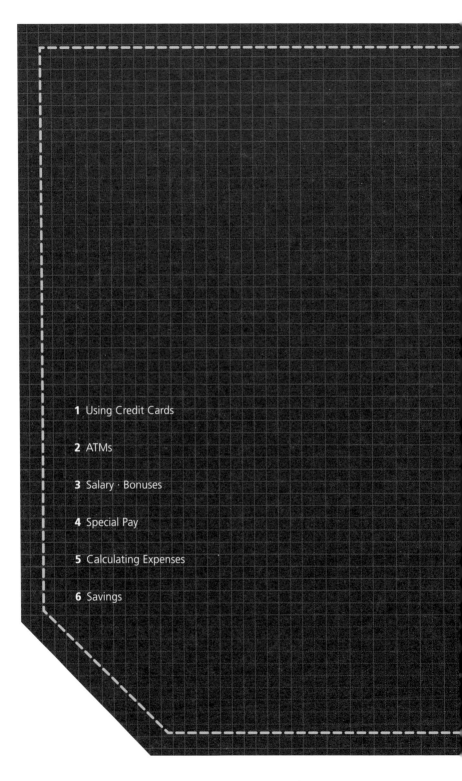

1 Using Credit Cards

2 ATMs

3 Salary · Bonuses

4 Special Pay

5 Calculating Expenses

6 Savings

CHAPTER 13

Money Matters

Using Credit Cards 01

Ⓐ 계산은 어떻게 하시겠습니까?
payment how would do
How would you like to pay?

Ⓑ 카드로 할게요.
by card will do
By card.

- 현금으로 하시겠습니까, 카드로 하시겠습니까?
  by cash would do by card would do
  Will you be paying by cash or card?

- 이 카드는 한도액이 초과됐습니다.
  this card limit amount over
  This card is over its limit.

- 카드로 계산할 수 있나요?
  by card can pay
  Can I pay by credit card?

- 현금으로 계산하면 추가 할인을 받을 수 있어요?
  by cash if pay additional discount can get
  If I pay with cash, can I get an additional discount?

Ⓐ 결제 어떻게 해 드릴까요?
payment how will do
How would you like to pay?

Ⓑ 3개월 할부로 해 주세요.
by three months installment please do
Please make it in three monthly installments.

몇 개월 할부로 할까요?
how many months installment may do
Over how many months would you like to pay?

지금은 무이자 할부 행사 기간입니다.
now no interest installment event period be
We are now running a no-interest special.

일시불로 해 주세요.
by single payment please do
I'll just pay all at once.

할부로 계산하면 수수료가 붙습니까?
by monthly installment if pay charge added
Is there a charge for monthly financing?

무이자 할부가 몇 개월까지 됩니까?
no interest installment by how many months possible
What is the maximum number of months for no-interest financing?

A 이번 달에는 카드비가 200만 원이나 나왔어요.
this month card payment amount even two million won came out
This month's credit card bill is two million won.

B 카드를 많이 쓰셨네요.
card much used
You used your credit card a lot.

카드비가 연체됐어요.
card payment overdue
My credit card payment is overdue.

카드대금이 빠져나가고 나면 남는 돈이 없어요.
card payment after slipping left money there not be
After the credit card payment went out, there is no money left.

신용카드가 있으면 현금서비스를 받을 수 있어요.
credit card if there be cash advance can get
If you have a credit card, you can use the cash advance service.

현금서비스를 받으면 수수료가 너무 비싸요.
cash advance if get charge too expensive
The fees for the cash advance service are too expensive.

요즘은 병원비도 카드로 계산할 수 있어요.
recently medical expenses by card can pay
These days you can even pay hospital bills with a credit card.

포인트가 많이 쌓이는 카드가 좋아요.
point much accumulated card like
I like credit cards that give you a lot of bonus points.

항공사 마일리지가 적립되는 카드를 만들어야겠어요.
airline mileage accumulated card should make
I need to make a credit card that gets mileage on airlines.

백화점 카드를 발급받으려면 어떻게 해야 돼요?
department store card if want to be issued how should do
How can I get a department store charge card?

카드비는 통장에서 자동이체 되게 해 주세요.
card payment from bank account automatic withdrawal let be done
Please make it so my credit card bills are automatically paid from my bank account.

결제일은 매달 25일로 해 주세요.
payment date every month 25th please do
Please make the payment date the 25th of each month.

카드 사용 내역이 SMS로 안내되는 서비스를 신청하고 싶어요.
card usage breakdown in SMS guiding service want to apply
I want to apply for my credit card statements to be delivered by SMS service.

카드 사용 내역은 인터넷 사이트에서 볼 수 있습니다.
card usage breakdown at Internet site can see
You can view a breakdown of your card usage on the Website.

ATMs 02

Using ATMs is a convenient way to deposit, withdraw, and transfer money. There are usually no fees for using your own bank's ATMs. The one exception being when you use them after business hours, in which case there is often a small charge. And there are even higher fees for using other banks' ATMs.

A **이 근처에 현금지급기 어디에 있어요?**
here near ATM where there be
Where is there an ATM near here?

B **1층 로비에 있어요.**
at first floor lobby there be
There is one in the first floor lobby.

현금이 없어서 ATM에 돈 찾으러 가요.
cash don't have to ATM to withdraw money go
I don't have any cash, so I'll have to find an ATM.

한일은행 ATM 어디에 있는지 아세요?
Hanil Bank ATM where there be know
Do you know where there is a Hanil Bank ATM?

A 이거 120만 원인데 ATM 가서 입금하고 오세요.
this 1.2 million won to ATM please go and deposit and come
This will be 1.2 million won. Please go to an ATM to make payment.

B 네, 알겠습니다.
yes understood
Alright.

ATM 가서 10만 원짜리 수표로 70만 원 찾아오세요.
to ATM go in 100,000 won bank notes for 700,000 won please withdraw and come
Please go to an ATM and get 700,000 won in 100,000 won bank notes.

지금 100만 원 입금했는데, 입금 확인 부탁 드립니다.
now one million won deposited deposit please check
I just deposited one million won; please check to make sure it went through.

잔액조회 해 보고 싶은데요.
balance check want to try to do
I would like to check my balance.

◌ **통장정리 하려면 어떻게 하죠?**
update bankbook if want to how do
How can I update my bankbook?

Ⓐ ATM으로 무통장 입금을 하려면 어떻게 해야 되죠?
with ATM without bankbook to deposit how should do
How can I use an ATM to make a deposit without my bankbook?

Ⓑ 이 기계는 출금만 되고 입금은 안 됩니다.
this machine only withdraw possible deposit not possible
This machine is only for withdrawals, not deposits.

◌ **현금인출기 어떻게 사용하는지 좀 가르쳐 주세요.**
ATM how to use please teach
Could you please teach me how to use an ATM?

◌ **이 기계는 수표는 안 되고 현금만 찾을 수 있어요.**
this machine check not possible only cash can withdraw
This machine has no bank notes; it only has cash.

◌ **이 기계는 5만 원권은 입출금이 안 되네요.**
this machine 50,000 won bill deposit and withdrawal not possible
This machine does not have any 50,000 won bills.

◌ **비밀번호가 갑자기 생각이 안 나네요.**
password suddenly not think
Suddenly I can't remember my password.

카드가 안 나와요.

card won't come out

My card won't come out.

만 원짜리가 한 장 덜 나왔어요.

10,000 won bill one sheet less came out

I am missing one 10,000 won bill.

편의점에 있는 ATM은 수수료가 좀 비싼 것 같아요.

at convenience store there be ATM charge a little seem expensive

The charges for the ATMs at convenience stores seem a bit expensive.

아파트 관리비 계좌이체 시키고 오겠습니다.

apartment maintenance cost will transfer and come

I'll go and send my apartment maintenance fees.

The Cash Receipt System

In Korea, when you buy something using cash, the employee will often ask "현금영수증 하시겠어요?" What they are actually asking is if you would like the purchase officially reported to government for tax purposes. According to the Korean cash receipt system, when a customer pays in cash and gives either a tax-save card or cell phone number, the store will issue a cash receipt and make a report of it to the national tax authorities. When doing year-end calculations for taxes, these purchases can be counted as deductions for individuals, and as business expenses for corporations.

Salary · Bonuses 03

There is a custom in Korea of buying one's parents a pair of red long underwear after having received one's first paycheck.

A 신입사원은 월급이 얼마쯤 돼요?
new employee monthly salary about how much
About how much do new employees make a month?

B 기본급 180만 원에 수당이 좀 나와서 250만 원쯤 받아요.
at base pay 1.8 million extra pay a little come out 2.5 million get
My base pay is 1.8 million won, but with extra pay I make average about 2.5 million won.

김민호 씨는 호봉이 나하고 얼마나 차이가 나지요?
Mr. Kim Minho pay grade with me how much differ
Mr. Kim Minho, what is the difference in our pay grades?

김 부장님은 연봉이 7,000만 원이 넘을 거예요.
manager Kim annual salary 70 million must be over
Ms./Mr. Kim probably makes over 70 million won per year.

월급이 세전 400만 원 정도인데 이것저것 공제하고 나면 실수령액은 얼마 되지 않습니다.
monthly payment before tax about 4 million won this and that after deducting actual take-home pay little be
My monthly salary is 4 million won before taxes, but after all the deductions, I take hardly anything home.

평사원은 기본급 150만 원에 실적에 따라 인센티브를 받게 됩니다.
normal employees base pay 1.5 million according to actual record incentive get
The base pay for normal employees is 1.5 million won, plus incentives received based on performance.

월급이 쥐꼬리만해요.
salary small as mice tail
My salary is just chicken feed.

한국에서는 금융업이 연봉이 제일 센 편입니다.
in Korea financial industry annual salary most strong sort of
In Korea, salaries are highest in the financial industry.

A 월급날이 언제예요?
payday when be
When is payday?

B 우리 회사는 25일이 월급날이에요.
our company 25th payday be
Our company's payday is the 25th.

우리 회사는 월급 수령일이 매달 20일입니다.
our company payday every month 20th be
Our company's payday is the 20th of each month.

월급날이 되려면 멀었는데 벌써 통장에 돈이 하나도 없네요.
payday to become be far already at in account no money be
Payday is still a long way off, but I already have no money in my account.

제 월급은 아내 통장으로 자동이체 됩니다.
my monthly pay to wife's account automatic transfer done
My monthly paycheck goes to my wife's account by direct deposit.

이번 달 월급명세서를 못 받았습니다.
this month paycheck not received
I didn't get a receipt for this month's paycheck.

A 월급 받으면 보통 어디다 돈을 많이 쓰세요?
when monthly pay if get where money a lot spend
When you get paid, where do you usually spend most of it?

B 문화생활하는 데 많이 쓰는 편이에요.
in enjoying culture much spend sort of
I tend to spend a lot on cultural activities.

생활비로 쓰고 나면 남는 게 없습니다.

as living expenses after spend left thing there not be

I have nothing left after living expenses.

올해 연봉이 5% 인상됐습니다.

this year annual pay 5% increased

Annual pay rose by 5% this year.

첫 월급을 받았습니다.

first monthly pay received

I received my first paycheck.

우리 회사는 연봉제라서 해마다 연봉 협상을 해야 합니다.

our company because of annual salary system every year salary must negotiate

Our company uses an annual salary system, so we have to renegotiate each year.

Year-End Adjustments

Year-end adjustments refers to the process by which the monthly taxes deducted over the course of a year are calculated. If they have been too high, an income tax return is given; if they have been too low, additional taxes are levied. During these calculations, exemptions can be granted for a certain portion of expenses for categories such as medical costs, education, donations, and credit card use. Foreigners residing in Korea may use the Year-End Adjustments Simplification Service (www.yesone.go.kr), where they can conveniently gather all the documentation for exemptions.

Income earned inside and outside Korea must be reported, and if you use the automated system in English (www.nts.go.kr/eng) you can do these calculations yourself, and then choose the correct option for reporting. Also, foreigners may dial 110 (Government Information Center) for help concerning year-end adjustments. And the tax office for each region also provides assistance through interpreters.

Special Pay 04

Ⓐ 이번 달 시간 외 근무 수당으로 얼마나 나왔어요?
this month overtime payment how much come out
How much overtime did you make this month?

Ⓑ 저는 이번 달에는 시간 외 근무 수당으로 30만원 받았어요.
I in this month for overtime payment 300,000 won got
I made 300,000 won in overtime this month.

우리 회사는 야근 수당이 얼마지요?
our company night overtime payment how much be
How much does our company pay for working nights?

우리 회사는 시간 외 근무 수당이 얼마나 돼요?
our company overtime payment how much
How much does our company pay for overtime?

시간당 만 원쯤 될 거예요.
per hour about 10,000 won may be
It's about 10,000 won per hour.

직급에 따라 달라요.
according to rank differ
It varies by rank.

시간 외 근무 신청서 작성했어요?
overtime work application drew up
Did you fill out a request for overtime?

특근 신청서 작성했어요?
extra work application drew up
Did you fill out a request for special work?

Calculating Expenses 05

When taking care of business expenses, most companies will accept handwritten receipts up to 50,000 won, but will expect credit card to be used for anything exceeding that.

A **비용 정산할 때 간이영수증은 얼마까지 인정이 되나요?**
when expense calculate handwritten receipt by how much admitted
When calculating expenses, what is the most expensive handwritten receipt accepted?

B **간이영수증은 비용이 5만 원 미만일 때만 사용 가능합니다.**
handwritten receipt expense only under 50,000 won can be used
You may only use handwritten receipts for expenses under 50,000 won.

현금영수증도 인정돼요?
cash payment receipt also admitted
Are cash receipts also accepted?

5만 원 이상은 카드로 결제하는 게 경비 처리하기 편합니다.
over 50,000 won pay by card expense settlement easy
For expenses over 50,000 won, paying by credit card makes calculations easier.

5만 원 이상의 현금 사용분에 대해서는 세금계산서가 있어야 비용 처리가 됩니다.

over 50,000 won about cash payment receipt for tax reduction should there be expense settlement possible

For cash payments over 50,000 won, you must have a tax receipt in order to be reimbursed.

카드 사용은 법인카드 사용분에 대해서만 전액 비용 처리가 됩니다.

credit card use only usage with company card total expense reimbursement possible

When using a credit card, only company cards qualify for full reimbursement.

접대비는 반드시 법인카드를 사용하여야 비용이 인정됩니다.

entertainment expenses surely company card should use expenses be approved

Entertainment expenses must absolutely be put on a company card.

개인 카드 사용분에 대해서는 업무용으로 사용한 것이 확인되는 경우에만 비용 인정됩니다.

about personal card use amount for business use only approved case expense be approved

When using a personal credit card, you will be reimbursed only in those cases where it can be confirmed it was used for business.

Savings 06

When you open a bank account in Korea, even if the balance is small, there are no fees. In fact, there are a variety of different financial products, all of which accrue interest. Even with a normal savings account, which makes deposits and withdrawals quite easy, you will earn a little interest, according to your balance. In addition, the government provides insurance up to 50 million won, so you would be reimbursed even if the bank were to fail.

Ⓐ 무엇을 도와 드릴까요?
what will help
How may I help you?

Ⓑ 계좌를 개설하러 왔는데요.
account to open came
I came to open an account.

오늘 통장을 하나 더 만들었어요.
today account one more made
I opened another account today.

통장을 개설하러 왔는데요.
account to open came
I came to open an account.

○ **계좌를 만들러 왔습니다.**
account to make came
I came to open an account.

○ **대출을 좀 받았으면 해서요.**
loan a little want to take out
I would like to take out a loan.

Ⓐ **어떤 상품으로 하시겠습니까?**
what product will make
Which product would you like?

Ⓑ **입출금이 자유로운 통장으로 하고 싶은데요.**
deposit and withdrawal free account want to make
I want an account that allows freedom to deposit and withdrawal.

○ **자유적립식 예금을 하나 들려고 합니다.**
free installment savings one intend to make
I want to open a free installment savings account.

○ **마이너스 통장을 만들고 싶은데요.**

credit line want to open

I want to open a line of credit.

○ **청약 통장을 만들고 싶은데요.**

subscription account want to open

I want to open a subscription account.

A 저금은 얼마나 하고 있어요?

savings how much are doing

How much are you saving?

B 집을 장만하려고 매월 150만 원씩 적금을 붓고 있습니다.

to buy house each month 1.5 million won installment saving depositing

I am saving 1.5 million won per month toward buying a house.

○ **다음 달이면 3년 만기 정기적금이 만기가 됩니다.**

by next month three-year maturity installment savings matured

Next month my three-year installment savings account reaches maturity.

○ **이번에 아파트를 장만하면서 은행에서 7,000만 원을 대출받았습니다.**

this time buying apartment from bank 70 million won loaned

When I recently bought my apartment, I took out a bank loan of 70 million won.

○ **목돈을 마련하려면 적금을 붓는 게 좋지요.**

a good chunk of money to make installment savings make good

If you want to save up a substantial sum of money, installment savings are good.

아파트를 분양 받으려면 청약 통장이 있어야 합니다.

apartment to be allotted subscription account should have

If you want to be allotted an apartment, you must have a subscription account.

무주택자가 장기주택마련 저축을 들면 소득공제를 받을 수 있어요.

non-home-owner longterm house subscription savings if open tax deduction can get

If you open a longterm savings account for first time home buyers, you can receive a tax deduction.

5,000만 원을 10년 동안 거치하시면, 1억으로 만들어 드리겠습니다.

50 million won for ten years if defer to 100 million won will make

If you are willing to defer your 50 million won for ten years, we can make it into 100 million won for you.

Caution

When reading numbers in Korean, don't stop at the commas.

Korean numbers are read with four zeros, not three. That is, larger numbers are counted from 10,000 instead of 1,000. For example, in Korean 100,000 is not read "one hundred thousand," but rather "ten ten thousand (십만 원)."

Vocabulary

Salaries and Wages

연봉
annual salary

월급
monthly pay

주급
weekly pay

시급
hourly wage

기본급
base pay/base salary

인센티브
incentive

상여금/보너스
bonus

임금협상 타결
pay settlement

지급내역
breakdown

근로소득세
an earned income tax

주민세
residence tax

공제내역
deduction breakdown

건강보험
health insurance

호봉
pay step/salary class

월급날
payday

실수령액
take-home pay

임금인상
wage increase/salary increase

임금동결
freezing of wages

임금협상
pay negotiation

월급명세서
payroll

고용보험
unemployment insurance

국민연금
national pension

실업급여
unemployment benefit

사업주
business owner

근로자
laborer/worker

고용주
employer

피고용인
employee

가입자
member

소득공제
deduction from one's income

연말정산
year-end tax adjustment

Savings

저축
savings

통장
bankbook

계좌
account

계좌 번호
account number

비밀번호
password

카드 번호
card number

예금
deposit/savings

적금/정기적금
installment savings

정기예금
fixed deposit/time deposit

주택 청약 예금
an apartment-application deposit

연금보험
annuity insurance

1 Local Buses

2 The Subway

3 Taxis

4 Driving

5 Parking

6 Car Problems

7 Traffic Accidents

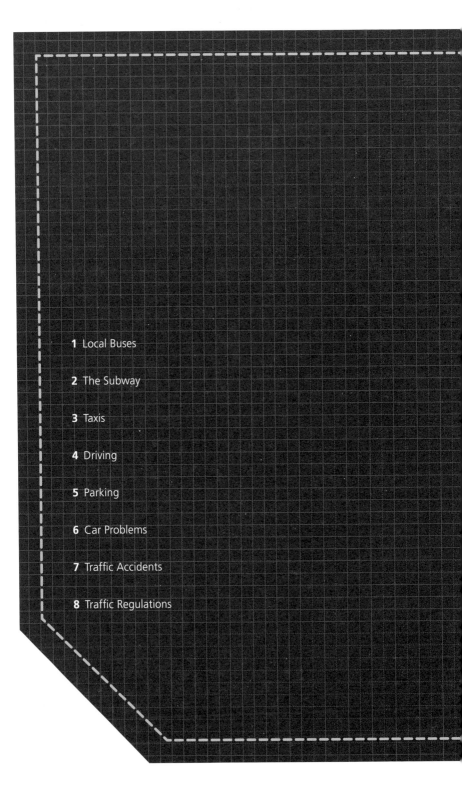

8 Traffic Regulations

CHAPTER 14

Local Transportation

Local Buses 01

There are many types of local buses including metropolitan, main route, and village buses. In major cities, including Seoul, there are bus-only lanes, making this a quicker way to reach your destination than by car.

A 이 버스 서울역에 가요?
this bus to Seoul Station go
Does this bus go to Seoul Station?

B 네, 서울역 갑니다.
yes Seoul Station go
Yes, it goes to Seoul Station.

신촌에 가려면 몇 번 버스를 타야 돼요?
to Sinchon to go what number bus should take
What number bus should I take to go to Sinchon?

이 버스는 공항에 안 갑니다.
this bus to airport not go
This bus does not go to the airport.

길 건너서 타세요.
street cross please take
Please get on across the street.

472번 버스를 타세요.
number 472 bus please take
Please take the 472.

다음 정거장에서 내리세요.
at next stop please get off
Please get off at the next stop.

두 정거장 더 가서 내리세요.
two stops more please go and get off
Please get off after two more stops.

인사동 가려면 어디서 내려요?
Insa-dong to go where get off
Where should I get off for Insa-dong?

저 내립니다.
I get off
I'm getting off.

문 좀 열어 주세요.
door please open
Please open the door.

이태원에 가려면 몇 정거장 더 가야 돼요?

to Itaewon to go how many stops more should go

How many more stops until Itaewon?

교통카드 어디서 충전해요?

transportation card where recharge

Where can I recharge my transportation card?

버스 요금 얼마예요?

bus fare how much be

How much is the bus fare?

교통카드를 안 찍고 내렸어요.

transportation card not put got off

I forgot to swipe my transportation card before I got off.

The Bus-Only Lane

You will see blue lanes either in the center or on the side of normal lanes; these are bus-only lanes. Many operate bus-only during peak traffic hours, but some are bus-only 24 hours.

The Subway 02

There are subway systems in Seoul, Busan, Daegu, Daejeon, and Gwangju. Seoul has a total of nine lines, with line No.1 running directly through the heart of the city. This line goes north as far as Uijeongbu and Dongducheon, west as far as Incheon, and south as far as Suwon and Cheonan. The Seoul subway system is also connected to the national railroad lines in the Gyeonggi and Chungcheong regions, making it an ideal means of transportation for those who work in Seoul and live either in or outside the Seoul metropolitan area.

A **인사동에 가려면 지하철 몇 호선을 타야 돼요?**
to Insa-dong to go subway which line should take
Which subway line should I take to get to Insa-dong?

B **지하철 3호선을 타세요.**
subway line No.3 please take
Please take line No.3.

압구정역에 가려면 여기서 2호선 타고 가다가 교대역에서 3호선으로 갈아타야 돼요.
to Apgujeong Station to go from here line No.2 take and at Gyodae Station into No.3 should transfer
If you want to go to Apgujeong Station, take line No.2 from here, then transfer to line No.3 at Gyodae Station.

종로3가역에서 내리세요.
at Jongno 3-ga Station please get off
Please get off at Jongno 3-ga Station.

4호선으로 갈아타려면 어디로 가야 돼요?
into line No.4 to transfer to where should go
Where should I go to transfer to line No.4?

A 다음 역이 무슨 역이에요?
next station which station be
What is next station?

B 다음은 교대역이에요.
next Gyodae Station be
The next station is Gyodae.

여기가 어디예요?
here where be
Where are we now?

내릴 역을 지나쳤어요.
to get off station passed
I missed my station.

지하철 노선도 어디 있어요?
subway map where there be
Where is there a map of the subway?

A 교보문고에 가려면 몇 번 출구로 나가요?
to Kyobo Bookstore to go to which number exit go out
Which exit should I take to go to Kyobo Bookstore?

B 4번 출구로 나가세요.
to number 4 exit please go out
Please go out the exit 4.

명동역 4번 출구에서 만나요.
Myeong-dong Station at number 4 exit let's meet
Let's meet at the exit 4 of Myeong-dong Station.

1번 출구에서 나와서 오른쪽으로 가면 박물관이 나옵니다.
from number 1 exit go out and to right side if go museum come out
If you go out exit 1 and turn right, you will see a museum.

그 백화점은 지하철역에 연결돼 있습니다.
that department store to subway station connected
The department store is connected to the subway station.

A 근처에 지하철역 있어요?

nearby subway station there be

Is there a subway station nearby?

B 사거리에서 왼쪽으로 가면 지하철역이 나와요.

at intersection to left side if go subway station come out

If you take a left at the four-way intersection, you will see a subway station.

여기서 제일 가까운 지하철역은 어디예요?

from here most near subway station where be

Where is the nearest subway station?

이태원에는 몇 호선이 다닙니까?

in Itaewon which line go around

Which subway line runs through Itaewon?

막차는 몇 시에 있어요?

last train at what time there be

What time is the last train?

첫차는 몇 시에 있습니까?

first train at what time there be

What time is the first train?

7호선은 몇 시까지 다닙니까?

line No.7 until what time go around

How late does line No.7 run?

Taxis 03

In Korea, there are two kinds of taxis: normal and deluxe. While the deluxe are more expensive, they also provide larger cars and better service. The regular taxis most often have a white sign on the top, while the deluxe have a yellow sign.

A 어디로 모실까요?
to where shall take
Where shall I take you?

B 이태원 갑시다.
Itaewon let's go
Let's go to Itaewon.

택시!
taxi
Taxi!

어디 가십니까?
where go
Where are you going?

청계천이요.
Cheonggyecheon be
To Cheonggyecheon, please.

올림픽대로로 해서 가 주세요.
via Olympic Highway please go
Please go via the Olympic Highway.

한남대교로 해서 가 주세요.
via Hannam Bridge please go
Please go over the Hannam Bridge.

A 저기 은행 앞에서 우회전 해 주세요.
there in front of bank please turn right
Please make a right turn in front of that bank.

B 네, 알겠습니다.
yes understood
Alright.

좌회전 해 주세요.
please turn left
Please turn left.

직진해 주세요.
please go straight
Please go straight.

좀 천천히 가 주세요.
a little slowly please go
Please go a bit slower.

빨리 좀 가 주세요.
fast a little please go
Please go a bit faster.

Ⓐ 좀 덥네요. 히터 좀 꺼 주세요.
a little hot heater please turn off
It's a bit hot. Please turn off the heater.

Ⓑ 네.
yes
Okay.

에어컨 좀 켜 주세요.
air conditioner please turn on
Please turn on the air conditioner.

라디오 소리 좀 줄여 주세요.
radio volume a little please turn down
Please turn down the volume.

창문 좀 올려 주세요.
window a little please raise
Please roll up the window.

창문 좀 내려 주세요.
window a little please lower
Please roll down the window.

A 횡단보도 앞에 세워 주세요.
in front of crosswalk please stop
Please let me off in front of the crosswalk.

B 네.
yes
Alright.

여기서 세워 주세요.
here please stop
Please let me off here.

저기 은행 앞에 내려 주세요.
there in front of bank please drop off
Please let me off in front of that bank.

아파트 안으로 들어가서 세워 주세요.
inside apartment go in and please drop off
Please let me off inside the apartment complex.

카드 결제 돼요?
credit card payment possible
Can I pay by credit card?

교통카드로 결제할 수 있습니까?
by transportation card can pay
Can I pay by transportation card?

Driving 04

Korean drivers tend to be a bit more aggressive than those in many other countries. Slower moving cars will often be pushed to speed up by honking horns and screaming drivers, but you should always simply ignore them and proceed at a safe pace.

A **끼어들기 할 때 깜빡이를 켜야지요.**

when cut in blinkers should turn on

You should turn on your blinkers before cutting into traffic.

B **아, 미안해요. 급해서 정신이 없었네요.**

ah sorry because busy out of mind

Oh, I'm sorry. I was in too much of a hurry.

여기는 일방통행 구역이네요.

here one-way area be

This is a one-way street.

커브 길에서는 추월하면 위험해요.

on curve road if pass dangerous

It is dangerous to pass on a curve.

우회전 할 때 오른쪽 깜빡이를 넣어야 합니다.

when turn right right side blinkers should turn on

You have to turn on your right blinker when making a right turn.

○ **정차할 때 비상등을 켜야지요.**

when stop car emergency light should turn on

When you stop, you have to turn on your hazard lights.

○ **언덕길에 주차할 때는 사이드 브레이크를 꼭 걸어놔야 돼요.**

at sloping road when park parking brake surely should put on

When parking on a hill, you absolutely have to use your emergency brake.

○ **1차선으로 가야겠어요.**

to first lane should go

I should go in the first lane.

○ **대리운전 좀 불러 주세요.**

driving service please call

Please call me a driving service.

A **얼마나 넣을까요?**

how much put in

How much would you like?

B **20리터 넣어 주세요.**

20 liters please put in

20 liters, please.

○ **가득 넣어 주세요.**

full please put in

Fill it up, please.

○ **3만 원어치 넣어 주세요.**

30,000 won worth please put in

Give me 30,000 won's worth, please.

경유차예요.
diesel car be
This is a diesel car.

경유로 주세요.
for diesel please give
Give me diesel, please.

고급유로 넣어 주세요.
for high grade oil please put in
Please put in high octane gas.

기름이 다 떨어졌어요.
gas all ran out
I'm all out of gas.

근처에 주유소 있습니까?
nearby gas station there be
Is there a gas station nearby?

5만 원 이상 주유하시면 기계 세차는 무료입니다.
over 50,000 won if refuel machine car wash free of charge be
If you put in over 50,000 won's worth, the automatic car wash is free.

A 손 세차 하는 데 얼마예요?
car hand wash how much
How much is it for a hand wash?

B 18,000원입니다.
18,000 won be
It's 18,000 won.

- **세차장은 어디에 있습니까?**
  car wash place where there be
  Where is the car wash?

- **실내 세차를 해야겠어요.**
  inside car wash should do
  I should also clean the inside of my car.

- **손 세차를 하고 싶은데요.**
  car hand wash want to do
  I would like to get a hand wash.

Parking 05

When visiting a company or office located in a large building, you can usually receive a parking voucher or stamp that will exempt you from paying parking fees.

A 주차비가 얼마예요?
parking fee how much
How much is parking?

B 30분에 2,000원이고, 그 다음부터는 10분에 1,000원입니다.
per 30 minutes 2,000 won after that per 10 minutes 1,000 won be
The first 30 minutes are 2,000 won, and it is 1,000 won for each additional 10 minutes.

주차비는 한 시간에 3,000원입니다.
parking fee per hour 3,000 won be
Parking is 3,000 won per hour.

두 시간까지 무료입니다.
up to two hours free of charge be
The first two hours are free.

입구에서 주차증을 뽑으세요.
at entrance parking card please pull out
Please get a parking ticket at the entrance.

○ 방문하는 회사에 가셔서 주차 확인을 받아 오세요.

visiting company go and parking stamp please get

Please go to the company you are visiting and get a parking stamp.

○ 5만 원 이상 물건을 구입하신 영수증이 있으면 2시간 무료 주차입니다.

over 50,000 won goods purchased receipt if there be two hours free parking be

If you have a receipt for a purchase of over 50,000 won, you get free parking for two hours.

○ 11시에 주차장이 문을 닫으니까 그 전에 차를 찾아 가세요.

at eleven o'clock parking lot door close before that car please get

The parking garage closes at 11 p.m., so be sure to get your car before then.

○ 주차증을 잃어버렸어요.

parking card lost

I lost my parking ticket.

○ 이 근처에 공영주차장 있어요?

near here public parking lot there be

Is there a public parking lot nearby?

A 발레파킹 돼요?
valet parking possible
Is there valet parking?

B 네, 됩니다. 키 주시고 들어가시면 됩니다.
yes possible key give and can go in
Yes, there is. You may give me your key and go inside.

여기 주차해도 됩니까?
here parking possible
May I park here?

A 월주차 정기권은 어디서 발급 받을 수 있습니까?
monthly parking permit from where issue can get
Where can I get a monthly parking permit?

B 주차관리소에 가시면 됩니다.
at parking station if go can
You may go to the parking management office.

한 달 주차비가 얼마예요?
one month parking fee how much
How much is parking per month?

한 달에 15만 원입니다.
per one month 150,000 won be
It is 150,000 won per month.

Car Problems 06

When you have a problem with your car, and you cannot drive it to a service center, if you call your insurance agency they will provide free towing within a reasonable distance. Most insurance agencies provide mobile lockout service, battery charging, and tire repair three to five times per year free of charge, so you can most often easily solve problems with a single phone call.

A **배터리가 방전된 것 같아요.**
battery seem discharged
I think my battery has died.

B **거기가 어디십니까?**
there where be
Where are you?

시동이 안 걸려요.
start not get
It won't start.

배터리가 나갔어요.
battery went out
The battery's dead.

타이어에 펑크가 났어요.
tire puncture happened
I have a flat tire.

차에서 연기가 납니다.
at car smoke happen
My car is smoking.

차에서 이상한 소리가 납니다.
at car weird sound happen
My car is making strange sounds.

엔진오일을 갈아야 됩니다.
engine oil should change
I have to change the oil.

오일이 새는 것 같습니다.
oil seem leak
I think it's leaking oil.

핸들이 잠겼습니다.
steering wheel locked
The steering wheel is locked.

와이퍼가 작동을 안 합니다.
wipers not work
The windshield wipers don't work.

- **차에 열쇠를 두고 내렸습니다.**
  in the car key left and got off
  I locked my keys in the car.

- **차 열쇠를 잃어 버렸습니다.**
  car key lost
  I lost my car keys.

- **근처에 카센터 있어요?**
  nearby car service center there be
  Is there a car center nearby?

- **아는 자동차 정비업체 있으면 소개 좀 해 주세요.**
  know car repair shop if there be please introduce
  If you know a good auto repair shop, please introduce me.

The Transfer System

In the Seoul-Gyeonggi area and in some other major metropolitan areas, there is a system of discounts in place when passengers transfer between or among city buses, village buses, and subways. Bus-bus and bus-subway transfers are possible, and prices are determined by distance, not by number of transfers. If you wish to receive a discount, you must place your card against the scanner/terminal before you exit the bus or subway. You must also get on the next bus or subway within 30 minutes. When you get on, place your card in front of the scanner, and you should hear a recording say "환승입니다," or "This is a transfer." This means you have received your discount. This does not apply, however, if you get back on a bus with the same number.

Traffic Accidents 07

If you call your insurance agency, usually a representative will arrive within 30 minutes. And the representative will take care of everything. But sometimes, particularly in the case of very minor accidents, it makes more sense for both parties to come to an agreement, exchange a small amount of money, and be done with it. When the accident is severe, however, and someone has been injured, you should call not only your insurance company but also 119 for paramedics.

A 접촉 사고가 났는데요.
fender bender happened
I had a fender bender.

B 계신 곳이 어디십니까?
there be place where
Where are you now?

교통사고가 났는데 좀 와 주시겠어요?
traffic accident happened please come
I had an accident, could you please send someone?

여기는 강남역 사거리 SM빌딩 앞이에요.
here Gangnam Station intersection SM Building in front be
I'm at the Gangnam Station intersection, in front of the SM Building.

여기가 어디인지 잘 모르겠어요.

here where well not know

I'm not sure where this is.

제 차 번호는 3219입니다.

my car number 3219 be

My license plate number is 3219.

A 죄송합니다. 제가 신호를 잘못 봤습니다.

sorry I signal wrong saw

I am sorry. I missed that signal.

B 어디 다치신 데 없으십니까?

where hurt spot there not be

Are you hurt?

앞차 뒷범퍼를 박았습니다.

front car back bumper crashed

I ran into the bumper of the car in front of me.

앞범퍼가 찌그러졌네요.

front bumper dented

The front bumper is dented.

라이트가 깨졌습니다.

light broken

The light is broken.

추돌사고가 났습니다.

rear-ender happened

I was rear-ended.

상대방이 중앙선을 침범했습니다.

opponent center line crossed over

The other driver came over the center divider.

차가 사람을 치고 달아났어요.

car a person hit and ran

There's been a hit-and-run.

Caution

Be aware of the seats reserved for persons with special needs.

On buses and subways there are seats reserved for the elderly, the infirm, and pregnant mothers. Even when these are empty, it is probably best not to sit in them. And, although it happens less now than in the past, it is also polite to give up even undesignated seats for those with special needs.

Traffic Regulations 08

If you are pulled over for a violation of traffic regulations, the police officer will ask to see your driver's license. Then, a few days later, when a ticket comes to your home, simply go to a nearby bank and pay the fine. When you are photographed breaking a violation, you will not be stopped but a ticket and photo will be delivered to your home, and you have to take care of this at the bank as well.

A 과속하셨습니다. 운전면허증 좀 보여 주십시오.
speeding driver's license please show
You were speeding. Please show me your license.

B 너무 급해서 그랬습니다. 한 번만 봐 주세요.
because too urgent did just once let it go
I am in such a hurry. Do you think you could forgive me just this once?

신호를 위반하셨습니다.
signal violated
You ran a red light.

잠시 음주 측정이 있겠습니다.
for a moment alcohol level measurement there be
We are testing for driving under the influence of alcohol.

◌ **차선을 위반하셨습니다.**
lane violated
You made a lane violation.

◌ **면허증을 집에 놓고 왔습니다.**
license at home left and came
I left my license at home.

◌ **안전벨트 미착용으로 벌금을 냈습니다.**
safety belt not wear fine paid
I paid a fine for not wearing my seat belt.

◌ **버스 전용 차로 위반으로 과태료가 나왔어요.**
bus-only lane due to violation penalty came out
I was fined for driving in the bus-only lane.

◌ **유턴 금지 구역에서 유턴하셨습니다.**
at U-turn banned area did U-turn
You made an illegal U-turn.

- 여기는 주정차 금지 구역입니다.
  here park stop prohibited area be
  This is a no-parking or stopping area.

- 운전 중에 핸즈프리 장치 없이 휴대전화를 사용하면 경찰의 단속에 걸립니다.
  while driving without hands free device cellular phone if use to the police check busted
  If you use a cell phone without a "hands free" device while driving, you may be pulled over by the police.

- 오늘부터 한 달간 교차로 꼬리물기를 집중 단속한대요.
  from today for one month stopping in intersection crackdown conducted
  For a month from today, there will be a crackdown on stopping in intersections.

Vocabulary

Traffic Signs

진입금지
Do Not Enter

우회전금지
No Right Turn

좌회전금지
No Left Turn

승용차통행금지
No Automobiles

유턴금지
No U-Turn

앞지르기금지
No Passing

주정차금지
No Parking or Stopping

주차금지
No Parking

최고속도제한
Limited Maximum Speed

최저속도제한
Limited Minimum Speed

1 Looking for Work

2 Applications

3 Interviews

4 Notification of Acceptance

5 First Day of Work

6 Introducing Colleagues

CHAPTER 15

Getting Hired and the First Day on the Job

Looking for Work 01

A 어떤 일을 하고 싶어요?
what kind work want to do
What sort of work would you like to do?

B 금융회사에 취직이 되면 좋겠습니다.
in finance company if get a job would be good
I would like to work at a finance company.

- 정부 기관에서 일할 수 있으면 좋겠어요.
at government organization if can work would be good
It would be nice if I could work for a government organization.

- IT 관련 회사에 들어가고 싶습니다.
IT related company want to enter
I want to enter a company that works in IT.

- 유통 관련 일을 하고 싶습니다.
distribution related work want to do
I want to do something in distribution.

- 대기업보다는 중소기업에서 일하고 싶어요.
rather than large enterprise at small or medium-sized enterprise want to work
I want to work at a small or medium-sized enterprise, rather than at a large company.

A **구인 광고는 어디에서 볼 수 있어요?**
recruiting advertisement from where can look
Where can I see the want ads?

B **구인구직 사이트에서 정보를 얻을 수 있을 거예요.**
on recruting Website information will be able to get
You will likely get information on a recruting Website.

모집 공고는 주요 일간지와 각 회사 홈페이지에서 볼 수 있습니다.
recruit public notice major daily newspapers and at each company's homepage can find
You can find recruitment ads in the major daily newspapers and on each company's homepage.

그 회사 인사부에 한번 연락해 보세요.
that company to HR once try to contact
Please try contacting that company's HR office.

홈페이지에 인사담당자 전화번호가 나와 있어요.
at homepage HR person in charge telephone number listed
The phone number of the person in charge of HR is listed on the homepage.

경력사원은 수시로 모집하고 있습니다.
experienced employee occasionally recruiting
They have open recruitment for experienced employees.

신입사원은 해마다 공채로 채용하고 있습니다.
new employee yearly through public employment employing
They publicly hire new employees each year.

대기업은 주로 연초에 신입사원을 모집합니다.

large enterprise mainly at the beginning of the year new employee recruit

Large companies generally recruit new employees at the beginning of the year.

Ⓐ 한림컨설팅에서 인턴사원을 뽑던데요. 지원해 보세요.

at Hollym Consulting internship hire try to apply

They are hiring interns at Hollym Consulting. You should apply.

Ⓑ 아, 그래요? 정보 고마워요.

ah so information thank you

Oh, really? Thanks for the tip.

지원서를 내 보세요.

application try to submit

Turn in an application.

홈페이지 공고란에서 봤어요.

homepage at public notice page saw

I saw the ad on your homepage.

인터넷에서 봤는데, 한림통상에서 통역과 번역을 담당할 사람을 뽑는대요.

on Internet saw, Hollym Trading interpretation and translation in charge person hire

I saw on the Internet that Hollym Trading is hiring someone to take charge of interpretation and translation.

우리 회사 마케팅부에서 계약직으로 일할 사람을 찾는데, 한번 지원해 볼래요?

our company in Marketing department to work as contractor look for once would apply

Our company is hiring contractors for the Marketing department; why don't you apply?

A 무역회사에 들어가고 싶은데 뭘 준비해야 할까요?

into trading company want to enter what should prepare

I would like to enter a trading company, so what should I prepare?

B 무역회사에 취직하려면 외국어에 능해야 되고 운전도 할 줄 알아야 합니다.

at trading company to get a job foreign language able should be able to drive

If you want to be hired at a trading company, you have to be good at foreign languages and at driving.

한국계 기업에 들어가려면 아무래도 한국어를 잘해야지요.

into Korean company to enter anyway Korean should do well

If you want to enter a Korean company, of course you should be good at Korean.

중국에 진출한 한국 기업에서는 한국어를 전공한 사람을 선호한대요.

into China entered Korean company person who majored in Korean prefer

I hear that Korean companies in China prefer people who have majored in Korean language.

관공서에는 들어가기가 어렵습니다.

into government and municipal offices to enter difficult

It is difficult to be hired at government and municipal offices.

Applications 02

Any discrepancies in the information provided on the application will result in a negative decision on hiring, so it is important that all applications be filled out truthfully and accurately.

A **이력서와 자기소개서 양식은 어떻게 구해요?**
resume and self introduction letter form how get
How can I obtain the forms for the resume and cover letter?

B **회사 홈페이지에서 지원서 양식을 다운 받으세요.**
from company's homepage application form please download
Please download the forms from the company's homepage.

홈페이지 채용 페이지에서 정보를 직접 입력하면 됩니다.
on homepage's recruit page information directly can type in
You can enter the information directly on the employment page of the homepage.

이력서와 자기소개서는 인사부 담당자 이메일로 보내세요.
resume and self introduction letter HR person in charge by email send
Please send your resume and cover letter by email to the person in charge of HR.

이력서와 자기소개서는 우편으로 보내세요.
resume and self introduction letter by mail send
Please send us your resume and cover letter by mail.

정해진 양식은 없습니다.
fixed form there not be
There is no set form.

각종 증명서는 추후에 제출하면 됩니다.
all sort of certificates later may hand in
The various certificates can be submitted later.

A 지원 마감일이 언제예요?
application deadline when be
When is the deadline for application?

B 다음 주 월요일이 접수 마감일입니다.
next week Monday receipt deadline be
Monday of next week is the deadline.

이력서는 언제까지 제출해야 돼요?

resume by when should hand in

By when must I submit my resume?

온라인으로 접수할 수 있습니다.

online can apply

You can apply online.

이번 달 17일까지 지원해야 합니다.

this month by 17th should apply

You should apply by the 17th of this month.

자기소개서는 A4로 한 페이지가 넘지 않게 쓰는 게 좋습니다.

self introduction letter A4 size one page not over write would be good

It is best if your cover letter does not exceed a single sheet of A4 paper.

Interviews 03

Ⓐ 대학에서 뭘 전공했습니까?
in college what majored
What did you major in at college?

Ⓑ 경영학과를 나왔습니다.
business administration department graduated
I graduated from the department of business administration.

경영학을 전공했습니다.
business administration majored
I majored in business administration.

대학교 때 한국어 번역 아르바이트를 해 본 경험이 있습니다.
when college Korean translation part-time work did experience there be
During college, I did part-time work in Korean translation.

AG 뉴욕지사에서 인턴으로 일한 경험이 있습니다.
at AG New York branch as intern worked experience there be
I worked as an intern at the New York branch of AG.

대학교 때 한국에 1년간 교환학생으로 온 적이 있습니다.
when college in Korea for one year as exchange student once came
In college, I spent a year abroad in Korea as an exchange student.

Ⓐ **저희 회사에 지원한 동기가 무엇입니까?**

to our company applied motivation what be

What motivated you to apply to our company?

Ⓑ **IT 분야에서 국제적인 경쟁력을 갖춘 HK 정보통신이야말로 영업 전문가가 되고 싶은 제가 할 수 있는 일이 많을 곳이라 판단되어 지원하게 되었습니다.**

in IT field global competitiveness equipped HK Information and Communications sales expert want to be I can do things a lot considered applied

I applied because I want to become a specialist in the IT field, a field in which HK Information and Communications is internationally competitive.

우리 회사에서 일하고 싶은 이유가 있습니까?

at our company reason to want to work there be

What is the reason you want to work at our company?

○ 고등학교 때부터 한림전자에서 일하는 게 제 꿈이었습니다.

from high school at Hollym Electronics to work my dream was

It has been my dream since high school to work at Hollym Electronics.

○ 저는 홍보 전문가가 되는 게 꿈이었습니다. 그 꿈을 세계적인 기업 한림에서 이루고 싶었습니다.

I PR expert to become dream was that dream global company at Hollym come true wanted

It is my dream to become a PR expert. I want to achieve that dream at Hollym, a world class company.

A 자신의 성격은 어떻다고 생각합니까?

yourself character what like think

How would you characterize yourself?

B 저는 성격이 털털하다는 말을 많이 듣습니다.

I personality free and easy a lot hear

I often hear that I am easygoing.

○ 자신의 장점과 단점에 대해 말해 보세요.

of yourself about strong and weak point tell me

Please tell us about your strengths and weaknesses.

○ 저는 성격이 꼼꼼해서 실수를 잘 안 하는 편입니다.

I character meticulous mistake scarcely sort of

I am fairly meticulous, so I make very few mistakes.

○ 책임감이 강한 편입니다.

responsibility strong sort of

I have a strong sense of responsibility.

A 원하는 연봉이 얼마인지 말해 보세요.
want annual salary how much tell me
Please tell us how much you would like to make.

B 회사 규정을 따르겠습니다.
company policy will follow
I will follow company policy.

우리 회사는 해외 출장이 잦은데 괜찮겠습니까?
our company business trip to abroad frequent will be alright
Our company has a lot of overseas business trips; will that be alright?

우리 회사는 밤샘 근무가 잦은 편인데 감당할 수 있겠습니까?
our company overnight work frequent will be able to cope with
At our company, we pull a lot of all-nighters; do you think you can handle it?

6개월간 수습 기간을 거쳐야 합니다.
for six months probation period should get through
You have to go through a six-month probationary period.

A 우리 회사에 입사했을 경우, 어떤 부분에서 회사에 기여할 수 있다고 생각합니까?

our company in case of entering into in which part to company can contribute think

If you do enter our company, where do you think you can contribute?

B 한국과 터키의 무역 교류에 도움이 되고 싶습니다.

Korea and Turkey's trade exchange want to help

I would like to help with trade and exchange between Korea and Turkey.

앞으로의 포부에 대해 말해 보세요.

hereafter about aspiration speak of

Please tell us about your future aspirations.

A 어느 부서에서 일하고 싶습니까?

at which department want to work

In which department would you like to work?

B 영업부에서 제 능력을 발휘하고 싶습니다.

in Sales dept. my ability want to show

I would like to display my abilities in the Sales department.

광고 홍보 관련 일을 하고 싶습니다.

PR related work want to do

I want to do something related to PR.

영업 일을 하고 싶습니다.

sales work want to do

I want to work in sales.

어떤 일이든지 맡겨 주신다면 최선을 다하겠습니다.

anything if give will do best

No matter what sort of work it is, I will do my best.

주어진 일에 최선을 다하는 사람이 되고 싶습니다.

for given work do best person want to be

I just want to be someone who does my best at whatever I am assigned.

연락드리겠습니다.

will contact

We will be in touch.

Notification of Acceptance 04

A 합격자 발표가 언제쯤 날까요?
successful applicants announcement about when happen
When will successful applicants be notified?

B 다음 주 금요일에 개별 연락한대요.
next week Friday individually get in touch
They say they will contact us individually next Friday.

합격자 발표가 언제예요?
successful applicants announcement when be
When will successful applicants be announced?

최종 합격자 발표는 다음 주 월요일입니다.
final successful applicants announcement next week Monday be
The final announcement of successful applicants goes out next Monday.

1차 서류심사에 합격한 지원자에 한하여 개별적으로 연락해 드릴 겁니다.
round one document screening passed applicants only individually will contact
We will contact only those who successfully pass the first round of document evaluations.

1차 합격자 명단은 홈페이지에서 확인하실 수 있습니다.
round one successful applicants list at homepage can find
You can check the list of round one passers on our homepage.

신입사원 최종 합격자 명단에서 이름을 확인하실 수 있습니다.
new employee from final passed list name can confirm
You can check for your name on the final list of new employees.

접수 번호를 입력하세요.
receipt number type in
Please enter your receipt number.

축하합니다. 합격하셨습니다.
congratulations passed
Congratulations! You passed.

A **합격 통지서는 어디로 받으러 가면 되나요?**
pass notification letter to where to receive may go
Where can I go to pick up my letter of acceptance?

B **합격 통지서는 인사관리부에서 받으시면 됩니다.**
pass notification letter from HR department may receive
You may receive your acceptance letter from the HR department.

신분증 가지고 내일 3시까지 인사과로 오세요.
ID bring tomorrow by three o'clock to HR please come
Please come to HR by 3 p.m. tomorrow, and be sure to bring identification.

내일 오전 9시까지 인사과로 와 주세요.
tomorrow morning by nine o'clock to HR please come
Please come to HR tomorrrow by 9 a.m.

First Day of Work 05

안녕하세요? 신입사원 스티브 잭슨입니다.
be well new employee Steve Jackson be
How are you? I am Steve Jackson, the new employee.

안녕하세요? 마케팅부 신입사원 마이클 김입니다.
be well Marketing department newcomer Michael Kim be
How are you? I am Michael Kim, a new employee in the Marketing department.

작년에 UCLA를 졸업했습니다.
last year UCLA graduated
I graduated from UCLA last year.

입사한 지 얼마 안 돼서 아직 모르는 게 많습니다.
entering company not long yet not know things a lot
I haven't been here long, and so there are still many things I don't know.

선배님들께 많은 지도 부탁 드립니다.
to seniors a lot of direction please ask
I will be asking you for a lot of help.

조직에 도움이 될 수 있는 사람이 될 수 있도록 노력하겠습니다.
to organization helpful person try to be
I will work hard to be someone who positively contributes to the organization.

홍보부에 배치 받았습니다.
at PR position placed in
I was assigned to the PR department.

마케팅부에서 일하게 되었습니다.
at Marketing department became work
I will be working in the Marketing department.

업무면에서도 부족한 부분이 많습니다.
in terms of work incomplete part a lot be
I still have a long way to go in terms of the job.

부족한 부분이 많지만 최선을 다하겠습니다.
incomplete part a lot will do best
I have a long way to go, but I will do my best.

편하게 대해 주세요.
easily please treat
Please be comfortable around me.

업무를 파악하려면 시간이 꽤 걸릴 것 같습니다.
job to grasp time fairly seem take
I think it will take quite a while before I really undertand the job.

Ⓐ **제 자리는 어디입니까?**
my seat where be
Where is my desk?

Ⓑ **마이클 씨 책상은 이 대리님 옆자리입니다.**
Michael desk next to supervisor Lee be
Michael, you are right next to Ms./Mr. Lee.

어느 컴퓨터를 쓰면 됩니까?
which computer may use
Which computer can I use?

신입사원 오리엔테이션은 언제입니까?
new employee orientation when be
When is the new employee orientation?

저는 첫인상이 좀 차가워 보이는 편인데 사실은 그렇지가 않습니다.
I first impression a little cold look sort of in fact not so
I may seem a bit cold at first, but I'm really not.

Introducing Colleagues 06

Ⓐ 이분은 저희 회사 기획실 이호민 실장님이십니다.
this person our company Planning dept. director Lee Homin be
This is Mr. Lee Homin from the Planning department.

Ⓑ 만나 뵙게 돼서 반갑습니다.
to get to meet glad
It's nice to meet you.

이분은 저희 부장님이십니다.
this person our manager be
This is my manager.

이 사람은 제 비서 김미선 씨입니다.

this person my secretary Ms. Kim Miseon be

This is my secretary, Ms. Kim Miseon.

이 친구는 마케팅부 김민호 씨인데, 제 고등학교 후배입니다.

this guy Marketing dept. Mr. Kim Minho my high school junior be

This is Mr. Kim Minho from Marketing; we went to the same high school.

저분은 SM전자의 김민준 전무님이십니다.

that person SM Electronics executive director Kim Minjun be

That is Mr. Kim Minjun, the Executive Director of SM Electronics.

Caution

Do not add "-씨" to your own name.

The suffix "-씨" is used to refer politely to someone the same age or younger; it should never be used when referring to oneself.

Resume

In Korean, a resume is referred to as either an "이력서" or an "입사지원서." Unlike many resumes in English, Korean resumes are written in chronological order. All fields must be filled out thoroughly and accurately.

입 사 지 원 서

지원부서		긴급연락처	휴대폰: 010-1234-5678 E-Mail: mk12@yaha.com

사 진	성 명	한글) 왕명 漢字) 王銘 영문) Ming Wang		
	주민등록번호	861012-6328712	성 별	남·여
	주 소	(120 - 750) 서울 서대문구 창천동 13-2		

학력	기 간	출신학교 및 전공	소재지	평점/평균
	2002년 3월 - 2005년 2월	북경 서북고등학교 졸업	북경	
	2005년 3월 - 2009년 2월	북경외국어대학교 한국어학과 졸업	북경	3.6/4.0
	2006년 9월 - 2007년 2월	연세대학교 한국어학당 한국어과정 수료	서울	

경력	기 간	근 무 지	직급
	2006년 9월 - 2007년 2월	연세대학교 한국어학당 행정실	조교
	2008년 7월 - 2008년 8월	베이징올림픽 자원봉사팀	통역 도우미
	2009년 1월 - 2010년 9월	베이징 여행사	가이드

병역					
필	복무기간				
	군별		병과		
미필사유					

개인사항				
	혈액형	O형	특기	노래
	신장	176cm	취미	운동

기능	
	O · A 활용가능 패키지
	MS Office (Word, Excel, PowerPoint), 한글

외국어	언어	사용정도	공인시험
	영어	상 · 중 · 하	TOEIC 820점
	한국어	상 · 중 · 하	TOPIK 6급 합격

Cover Letter

In Korean, a cover letter is referred to as "자기소개서." It most often includes information regarding one's family background, personality, reasons for applying, and plans for one's future at the company.

자 기 소 개 서

성장과정	모두들 영어를 고집할 때, 저희 부모님은 어릴 때부터 저에게 한국어를 배우게 하셨습니다. 덕분에 저는 초등학교 때부터 한국인 교회에서 운영하는 한글학교에 다니면서 한국어와 한국 문화를 배웠습니다. 한국어와 일찍이 인연을 맺은 저는 대학에서도 한국어학과를 선택하였습니다. 그리고 언어란 그 나라의 역사와 문화를 알고 그 바탕 위에서 이루어져야 한다는 생각에, 대학 3학년 재학 중 1년 간 교환학생으로 한국대학교에서 수학을 하였습니다. 그리고 복학 후 2011년 2월에 학위를 취득하였습니다.
성격 및 장단점	저는 책임감이 강하고 성실하며 새로운 환경에 잘 적응하는 편입니다. 매사에 긍정적이고 약간은 내성적이지만 주변 사람들을 배려하고 부드러운 분위기를 형성하는 것이 저의 장점이라 할 수 있습니다. 내성적인 성격은 오랜 유학생활로 새로운 사람들을 많이 접하면서 점차 어떤 환경에서도 사람들과 잘 어울릴 수 있는 성격으로 바뀌었습니다. 또 다른 제 단점은 남의 부탁을 잘 거절하지 못하는 것입니다. 그래서 부탁 받는 일에 저의 일까지 하느라 고생한 적이 많습니다. 저는 단점이 무엇인지 스스로 알고 노력하면 얼마든지 장점으로 바꿀 수 있다고 생각합니다. 단점을 아는 것, 그리고 그것을 고쳐 가는 것은 진정 자신을 사랑하는 일이라 생각합니다.
지원동기	한국은 중국과의 교역에 있어 지난 1992년 정식 수교 체결이후 수출은 7배가 증가하였지만, 한국 상품의 중국 내수 시장 공략이 미흡하고, 중국 시장 내 점유율과 경쟁력은 점점 하락하고 있습니다. 한국 상품이 중국 시장 내의 점유율과 경쟁력을 보강하기 위해서는 그 만큼 중국에 대해서 잘 알고 이해하는 인재가 필요하다고 생각합니다. 어려서부터 한국에 대해 배워 왔고 중국과 한국 간의 무역에 대해 공부해 온 저는 그 일을 잘 하리라는 믿음이 있어 귀사에 지원하게 되었습니다.
입사후포부	저에게 귀사에서 일할 기회가 주어진다면 아직까지는 경험이나 지식이 부족하지만 새로운 각오로 지금까지 배웠던 것과 경험을 토대로 열심히 노력할 것입니다. 저는 제가 완벽하게 준비된 인재라 생각지는 않습니다 하지만 채워야 할 빈자리가 있기에 꿈을 꿀 수도 있다고 생각합니다. 귀사의 미래를 짊어지고 나갈 수 있다는 자신감으로 제 꿈을 펼칠 수 있는 기회를 갖고 싶습니다.

Vocabulary

Applications

가족 관계
family

학력
education

경력
experience

특기
expertise/special skills

자격증
certificates/licenses

생년월일
birthday (year/month/day)

증명사진
photograph

희망 부서
desired department

희망 연봉
desired salary

졸업
graduation

졸업 예정
expected date of graduation

수료
completion

Appearances

준수하다
refined/elegant

잘생겼다
good-looking

못생겼다
ugly/bad-looking

훤칠하다
strapping/tall and slender

통통하다
plump/chunky

뚱뚱하다
fat

날씬하다
thin

말랐다
skinny

복스럽다
plump/cherubic

귀엽다
cute

험상궂다
stern/grim

곱상하다
fine

샤프하다
sharp

예쁘다
pretty

멋있다
fashionable/cool

단정하다
neat/tidy

세련됐다
sophisticated

촌스럽다
unsophisticated/unrefined

Personality

꼼꼼하다
meticulous

치밀하다
detail-oriented/meticulous

털털하다
easygoing

덤벙대다
reckless

차분하다
levelheaded

밝다
bright/pleasant

명랑하다
bright

깔끔하다
fastidious/neat

지저분하다
messy/dirty

부지런하다
diligent

성실하다
sincere/earnest

게으르다
lazy

칠칠맞다
sloppy

시원시원하다
outgoing/up front

조용하다
quiet/reserved

내성적이다
introverted

외향적이다
extroverted

적극적이다
positive

소극적이다
passive

긍정적이다
positive/optimistic

부정적이다
negative/pessimistic

어둡다
dark/gloomy

책임감이 있다
responsible

자기중심적이다
self-centered

사회성이 있다
sociable

현실적이다
practical

의지력이 약하다
weak-willed

창의적이다
creative

협동심이 부족하다
uncooperative

패기 있다
ambitious/driven

잘난 척하다
arrogant

겸손하다
humble

Appendix

Korean Holidays

신정 New Year's Day (January 1)

People exchange New Year's greetings and cards, but many people do not consider this as important as the first day of the lunar New Year since it is not a traditional holiday.

설날 Lunar New Year's Day (Lunar January 1)

This may just be the most significant holiday of the year, and its celebration lasts for three days. Some people still wear traditional clothing, and after first paying tribute to their ancestors before breakfast, wish their relatives and everyone they meet good luck in the coming year. On this day, rice cake soup (떡국) is served for breakfast, after which some families gather and play various traditional games.

삼일절 Independence Movement Day (March 1)

This day commemorates the independence movement that began on March 1, 1919 against Japanese colonial rule.

석가탄신일 Buddha's Birthday (Lunar April 8)

This day celebrates the birth of Buddha. On the night before this holiday, street parades with multi-colored lanterns are held, while bright lanterns are lit in all the temples.

어린이날 Children's Day (May 5)

The holiday was originally celebrated on May 1, but was later moved to May 5. Parents often give presents to their children as well as spend time with them.

현충일 Memorial Day (June 6)

This day pays tribute to and remembers all those brave soldiers who sacrificed their lives for their country.

광복절 Liberation Day (August 15)

This day celebrates Korea's liberation from Japanese rule, which lasted 36 years. Many events take place throughout the country including parades and fireworks.

추석 Thanksgiving Day (Lunar August 15)

Together with the lunar New Year's Day, it is one of the most important traditional holidays, and is also celebrated for three days. Traffic congestion should be expected on all the highways since many people head for their hometowns. On the other hand, Seoul is pleasantly relieved of its population and congestion, just as it is during the lunar New Year's holidays.

개천절 National Foundation Day (October 3)

This day commemorates the mythical Dangun's founding of the first state on the Korean Peninsula in 2333 BC.

성탄절 Christmas (December 25)

As in many other countries of the world, the birth of Christ is celebrated on this day and people exchange cards and gifts.

Useful Phone Numbers

Fire Department and Ambulance 119
(Including traffic accidents)

Crime 112

Local Telephone Number Information Center 114

BBS 1588-5644
(Volunteer service for interpretation for 16 languages 24hours/7days)

Helpline for Foreign Taxpayers 1588-0560

Travel Information 1330

Useful Websites

Korea Immigration Service
http://www.immigration.go.kr

Foreign Workers Service
http://www.eps.go.kr

Reservations for Hotels in Korea and Overseas
http://www.hoteljoy.com

Foreign Taxpayers Advocate Service
http://www.nts.go.kr/eng

Seoul Global Center
global.seoul.go.kr

Korea Tourism Organization
http://www.visitkorea.or.kr

Property Rentals
http://www.bluebirdnest.com
http://www.nicerent.com